What Makes Childminding Work?
A Study of Training for Childminders

What Makes Childminding Work?
A Study of Training for Childminders

by Elsa Ferri

ISBN 0 902 817 86 8

Published by the National Children's Bureau
8 Wakley Street
London EC1V 7QE
Telephone 071 278 9441

Typeset, printed and bound by Saxon Printing Ltd, Derby.

The National Children's Bureau was established as a registered charity in 1963. Our purpose is to identify and promote the interests of all children and young people and to improve their status in a diverse and multiracial society.

We work closely with professionals and policy makers to improve the lives of all children but especially children under five, those affected by family instability and children with special needs or disabilities.

We collect and disseminate information about children and promote good practice in children's services through research, policy and practice development, publications, seminars, training and an extensive library and information service.

Contents

vi

Acknowledgements

Many people have contributed to the study described in this book. These include the childminders and parents in Bracknell and Waltham Forest who gave so much of their time to talk to us, as did the social services workers in the two areas and the staff of National Children's Home Childminding Centre in Bracknell. Our gratitude and appreciation go to all of them.

Charmaine Pereira was a valued member of the research team for the duration of the study, and played a major part in designing the research instruments, undertaking the fieldwork and analysing the observation data. Thanks are also due to David Berridge for his support throughout the project and for his constructive comments on the draft report. To those who provided secretarial and administrative help, thanks are also extended; in particular, Ebah Eshun and Val Bull who word-processed the final manuscript, Sarah Brown and Gary Armitage for their contribution at earlier stages, and Edward Topham who printed the original report.

Finally, we wish to express our gratitude to the Department of Health for providing the financial support which made the study possible.

December 1991

1. Introduction

'We're only mums looking after other people's children.'

'It's a professional job – children's lives are at stake.'

These contrasting statements were made by two women engaged in exactly the same kind of work. They were among the participants in a study, carried out by the National Children's Bureau, of how practising childminders have responded to changes in what is by far the most common form of day care outside the home for pre-school children in Britain. The most recently published figures indicate that more than twice as many under-fives are cared for by registered childminders than by public and private nurseries combined (Melhuish and Moss, 1991). In addition, childminders also look after large, but unknown, numbers of school age children whose parents' working hours do not coincide with the normal school day.

Childminding by kin, friends and neighbours is probably as old as human society itself. Its origins in the extended family and in the local community are echoed in the words of the first practitioner cited above. These portray childminding as an activity commensurate with the primary care-giving and nurturance which, in our culture, is conventionally provided in a domestic setting by mothers. The second quotation, however, contains an alternative view of childminding which, through its contribution to children's welfare and development, is seen to merit the occupational status accorded to others who work with the youngest members of our society.

Which of these very different perspectives represents the reality of childminding in Britain today? A review of the changes which have taken place over the past 25 years or so would suggest, at first sight, a gradual but consistent shift in the direction of formalising child-minding in such a way as to reinforce the image of an emergent occupation. Various measures have been taken by the public authorities responsible for childminding to encourage would-be practitioners to comply with the legal requirement to register, to introduce more rigorous registration procedures and to offer a range of support services to practising minders. These moves have been matched by vigorous efforts on the part of local and national grassroots organisations to establish standards in relation to the work undertaken, and to ensure that it receives appropriate reward and recognition.

Perhaps the most radical and potentially significant change, however, lies in the introduction of training for childminding. The importance of training has long been unquestioned in other fields of work with children, such as health, education and the institutional day care setting of the nursery – the pursuit of courses leading to recognised qualifications is an established requirement for entry into these areas of employment. Yet it is only recently that the notion of training as relevant to childminding has received serious attention. The reasons for the long neglect and the emergent interest lie, as we shall see, in the historical background to childminding and to the policies of successive governments regarding day care for young children. But it is immediately clear that the application of training to a traditionally informal activity, conducted in the domestic setting of the provider, raises, if not a paradox, then at least a number of important questions. What are the aims and objectives of training in such a context? What should it consist of and how should it be delivered? Above all, perhaps, what is its impact on the way childminding is undertaken?

Such weighty questions as these point to training as a key issue in exploring how childminding operates in our society today and, in particular, how it is changing. It was for this reason that childminder training was adopted as the focus for the study reported in this book. In the following chapters we shall examine in some detail the role of training in relation to significant aspects of childminding in action. Before doing so, however, it is important to consider the historical and structural context in which childminding in Britain has developed, and to look at recent social trends which make a study of this kind particularly timely.

The legislative context

According to the official definition embodied in the first legislation governing the activity, a childminder is a person who, for reward, looks after a child under five, to whom she (or he) is not related, in her own home and for more than two hours a day. Under the most recent legislation, the Children Act 1989, the age limit in respect of minded children was extended to include all those under eight years of age.

The underlying approach to public involvement in this field of day care is captured in the title of a recent review of the legislative history of childminding, in which it is referred to as the 'unobjectionable' service (Owen, 1989). Although childminding, as a community-based day care activity, has existed for centuries, it was only 40 years ago that the first attempt was made to regulate it through legislation. Even then, clauses stating that childminders, as defined above, must register with their local health authority, appear to have been included almost as an afterthought in the 1948 Nurseries and Childminders Regulation Act, which had as its main target the regulation of factory and other private nurseries.

As Owen (op. cit.) points out, the policy stance towards child-minding was essentially non-interventionist, indicated by the following quotation from the 1948 parliamentary debate:

'We do not want in any way to interfere with the kindly relative or friend who looks after one or two children while the mother is at work...we do not think much harm can come to children looked after by friends and relatives in this way. We want to distinguish here between the good neighbourliness, the kind of services relatives provide, and the people that are going into childminding as a business.' (Hansard, 1948, 451, col.521)

It is interesting to note the distinction drawn in the above statement between providers offering childcare on a 'good neighbour' basis and those whose motives were perceived as economic – and hence implicitly suspect. This ambiguity surrounding the notion of childminding as informal care or as an occupation continues to permeate its whole operation, as we shall see time and again in the following pages.

During the next 20 years or so, childminding continued to expand as the major source of day care for working parents. Amendments to the law were included in the 1968 Health Services and Public Health Act, which increased the powers of local authorities in relation to the registration of childminders. However, this did little to alter the intrinsic weakness of a legislative framework which was rooted in the concept of *protection* from harm rather than the *promotion* of high quality care. Thus, registration requirements focused on the safety aspects of the premises concerned, and the notion of the childminder as a 'fit person'. Fitness, however, was defined only in terms of the *absence* of negative indicators such as a conviction for child abuse or disqualification from fostering or adoption, rather than the *presence* of any positive qualifications for the tasks of childcare. The amendments thus did little to create a framework for the provision of a high quality, publicly regulated service; a deficiency which has been the subject of sustained criticism, both from the local authority workers responsible for childminding, and from grassroots organisations of practitioners (Association of Advisers for Under Fives, 1980; National Childminding Association, 1979; 1984).

Twenty years on, the Children Act 1989 introduced some further modifications to the law relating to childminding. Registration could now be suspended if the quality of care was thought to be 'seriously inadequate'. The guidance issued in respect of implementation of the new legislation also sought to provide a more positive definition of 'fitness' for the task at hand (DH, 1991). The ensuing list of attributes included, in addition to the earlier negative indicators, previous experience or qualifications in work with young children or people with disabilities or the elderly, plus personal qualities such as 'ability to provide warm and consistent care' and 'commitment and knowledge to treat all children as individuals and with equal concern'. For the first time issues of race, religion and culture were also specifically referred to as important aspects of the *quality* of care, and local authorities were instructed to have regard to the representativeness of ethnic groups in recruiting childminders. This was an important step forward in a multicultural society in which the services available to minority ethnic groups are particularly unsatisfactory. A number of studies have highlighted the inadequate supply of childminders from such groups and the problems experienced by Black families in finding satisfactory day care (for example, Community Relations Commission, 1975; Jackson and Jackson, 1979; Mayall and Petrie, 1983).

Overall, however, the new legislation could not be seen as representing a major shift of policy in the direction of a more assertive stance on the subject of quality in the childminding service.

The preamble to the list of indicators referred to above stated merely that 'the local authority should have regard to these points when considering whether someone is fit to look after children aged under eight'. It was thus left to local authorities to decide what this should mean in practice – and how properly to *assess* whether or not someone possessed the qualities listed as desirable.

It is, however, not altogether surprising that the new legislation stopped short of public intervention to establish and ensure a high quality childminding service. The current policy position is in tune with a dominant ideological perspective which, as we shall see, emphasises *parental* responsibility and power in respect of the care arrangements made for children. It is also consistent with the perception of childminding as substitute mothering rather than skilled work – a point to which we shall also return later.

The local authority framework

Responsibility for childminding, originally vested with local health authorities, was allocated in 1970, under the Local Authority Social Services Act, to the newly-created social services departments. It is interesting to note that this move transferred day care provision from the administrative framework of the universal health service to the selective area of social welfare, a change which, as we shall see, was not without significance for the development of childminding. At this point, it is sufficient to point out that it reinforced the existing bias towards the *protective*, as opposed to the *promotional*, aspect of public intervention in the field of day care (Lane, 1980).

The nature of the social services role in relation to childminding also reflects a dualism in terms of the public and the private aspects of the service. As we have seen, the local authority has a legal duty to register childminders, and, under the 1989 Children Act, carry out inspections of their premises at least once a year, as well as having powers to cancel registration. It is here, however, that official public concern with childminding, as an activity, effectively ceases. The local authority has no formal responsibility towards childminders as *workers*. Minders are regarded as self-employed, and are thus normally expected to negotiate their own terms and conditions with the parents who place their children with them. An exception to this is the increasing number of childminders with whom local authorities are placing children in defined categories of need – either as a result of the unavailability, or perceived inappropriateness, of nursery provision. A range of schemes exist, whereby childminders become salaried employees of the social services department, or are paid all or part of their fees by the local authority (Ferri and Birchall, 1987). Under normal circumstances, however, social services departments have no legal responsibility for childminding arrangements, either to minders or to parents, with the onus resting on the latter to seek out the type of day care arrangement that they want.

The ambiguity of the local authority role is deepened by the *empowering* aspects of the relevant legislation, which, together with a series of central government guidelines, permit – and even encourage – social services departments to extend their involvement with childminding by providing a range of advisory and support services for childminders, including training courses. In practice, the nature and level of these services vary enormously from one area of the country to another, no doubt reflecting the differing priority attached to childminding in a department with a competing range of statutory duties. An initial review in our programme of research in this field showed, for example, that among a sample of local authorities known to be in the forefront of provision of childminding support services, the ratio of advisory staff to minders ranged from one to 25 to one to 225 (Ferri and Birchall, op. cit.).

The underlying aims of such strategies, as contained in a series of official guidelines, have been expressed in very general terms as seeking to improve the standards and status of childminding. It might well be argued that this is somewhat at odds with a policy of limited statutory intervention, which has been criticised as a major obstacle to developing a service which guarantees high quality and enjoys high esteem. It also introduces a certain ambiguity into the work of the social services staff, whose supervisory and inspectorial functions in respect of the legislation are thereby uneasily blended with a supportive or 'befriending' role, in the form of home visiting, providing toys and equipment loan facilities, drop-in centres and so on. Most significantly, however, from the perspective of the current study, the foregoing pages suggest that the approach of the public authorities to childminding, at both national and local level, raises questions rather than answers concerning the purpose of childminder training.

Grass roots movement

Another significant ingredient in this complex scene is the grass roots pressure for change, which has come from organised groups of childminders themselves. Starting from local associations which came together for the purposes of self-help and self-support, the practitioners' voice has been vigorously orchestrated by the National Childminding Association since its inception in 1977. An indication of the organisation's success in seeking to coordinate the interests of childminders lies in the growth of its membership, from fewer than 5,000 in 1980 to more than 30,000 in 1989 – almost half of all registered minders. The official recognition it has received as a body concerned with the status and standards of childminding is witnessed by the fact that it was one of the main recipients of central government funds paid to voluntary agencies to develop new initiatives in services for pre-school children – initiatives which included the provision of training courses for childminders (Ferri and Stern, 1987; Van der Eyken, 1987).

The international significance of the grass roots movement in the field of childminding – or family day care as it is more widely known in other countries – is evidenced by the formation in 1987 of the International Family Day Care Organisation, in which the British National Association played a major part.

The wider social context

Childminding is acquiring an increasing importance in our society, a trend which highlights the serious paucity of research on this type of day care provision. The reason for its growing significance lies in the rapid and dramatic changes which the last few years have witnessed in the field of women's employment and in the related area of child-care.

The dawn of the 1990s in Britain has been accompanied by an unprecedented surge of interest in the subject of day care for young children. It has long been evident that, as far as the supply of publicly-funded services is concerned, this country lags far behind most of its European neighbours, and has never come near to satisfying parental demand for provision (for example, Bone, 1977; Hughes and others, 1980). Until now, however, virtually the only voices raised in protest at this situation have been those of long-running campaigns by frustrated would-be consumers of day care services, and of researchers and others concerned with the welfare and support of children and families. Perhaps for the first time in our history, the need for a major expansion of provision is now being articulated by the hitherto silent ranks of government and employers.

This novel state of affairs has been created by the 'demographic time bomb' – a phrase which, in the space of a year or so, has become almost a cliché. Its significance is that, as a result of reduced birth rates in the recent past, an estimated one and a half million fewer young people will be entering the labour market in the decade up to the year 2000 than in the previous 10 years. In order to meet this serious shortfall of workers in a country already inferior to most of its competitors in terms of trained personnel, the economy is turning to mothers – especially those with very young children – as the main untapped source of alternative skilled labour. Despite the continuing rise in the number of working mothers over the past four decades, the overall rate of employment is considerably lower amongst those with children under school age (28 per cent) than it is for all mothers with dependent children (49 per cent) (Cohen, 1988).

In order to facilitate the re-entry of mothers into the labour market, there is now a widely acknowledged need for a substantial increase in organised day care provision, and for other measures which will enable women to combine the demands of work and family. Hardly a day now passes without media reports of employer-led initiatives in the form of workplace nurseries, childcare vouchers, career break schemes and so on, together with, albeit modest, fiscal changes of benefit to some working mothers.

However, before heralding these developments as signalling a peaceful, and astonishingly speedy, revolution in the British child-care scene, it would be prudent to consider a number of significant points. The first is that the impetus for this change has been *economic*; it has not been born out of a principled concern for the interests of children, families or gender equality. Day care provision has been recognised as a necessary condition for achieving the economic goal of attracting mothers into the workforce. It is pertinent to note that no such policy was in evidence in the preceding decades, which nonetheless witnessed a steady, dramatic increase in rates of maternal employment. Only in periods of national emergency – particularly during the Second World War – have public measures been taken to support and facilitate women's employment by the provision of day care services. The huge expansion of day nursery places during the war years was swiftly reversed after hostilities ceased and women were encouraged to retreat back to the domestic hearth. Even with the modest increase in public provision since the early 1970s, the total number of places in local authority nurseries is still less than half what was available at the end of the Second World War. It would not be overly sceptical, therefore, to adopt a cautious approach to current developments, at least from the perspective of the needs of children and families. Despite the advances and achievements of the feminist movement over the past 20 years or so, it would be unwise to assume that women – always a 'moveable feast' in terms of the exigencies of the labour market – will necessarily continue to benefit from public policies aimed at supporting their dual roles as workers and mothers.

We live in an age of rapid change and uncertainty in terms of economic, social and political trends. Demographic forecasting is a medium-term exercise; the structure of our population could change significantly in the not too distant future. In the shorter term, the imminent arrival of the single European market, with the attendant increase in labour mobility, may have an unpredictable impact on the employment situation of women in different regions, as may one of the consequences of the so-called 'peace dividend' in the shape of large scale military force reduction and its impact upon the labour market.

Another crucial point to be made in respect of the current situation is that the explicit recognition by several government departments of the gap in day care provision has not been accompanied by any policy committed to filling it through publicly-funded services. In other words, there has been no significant departure from the traditional position in Britain that the state has no interventionist role to play in the relationship between work and family life and, as such, assumes no responsibility for the care of children of working parents. Instead, the governmental approach is one of encouraging, rather than providing for, an expansion in day care provision, which continues to be viewed as a matter for private arrangement. The targets of the Government's exhortations in this matter are the employers, to whom it is turning as the main potential contributors to meeting the need.

Before considering what this is likely to mean as far as the development of day care services is concerned, it is important to

examine some of the values and assumptions which underpin this
official policy stance. Perhaps the most significant of these can be
expressed in the statement that Britain is not, and never has been, a
particularly child-centred society, in terms of the collective responsibility taken for children and the quality of their lives. The ensuing
policy position – and it is important to stress that policy is as clear in
its absence as in its presence – is particularly evident in relation to the
youngest members of society, that is, children below the age of
compulsory schooling. It can be seen to rest upon an ideological
perspective which stresses both the *responsibility* and the *privacy* of
the family in respect of how children are nurtured.

Responsibility of mothers

The responsibility of the family as far as childcare is concerned
would be more accurately described as the responsibility of the
mother. It is almost stating the obvious to point out that the current
childcare dilemma has been recognised only in the context of the
employment of *women*. As Moss (1990) has noted:

'The belief that women have the main responsibility for children pervades
every aspect of current discussion and developments. The issue is defined as
helping mothers cope with their family responsibilities.'

Thus, the very real economic and social changes which have taken
place in women's lives as increasing numbers have entered the labour
market have not had a corresponding impact on the patriarchal
ideology which casts them in the role of primary caregivers. The
effect of increased employment opportunities has not so much
transformed the mother's role as bolted on another component. As a
result, employed mothers are now under pressure to fulfil the triple
tasks of external work, child rearing and home management, despite
– or perhaps because of – the somewhat chimerical impact on the
domestic scene of the 1980s 'new man'. A number of studies here and
in the United States have shown that, even in families in which both
partners are in full-time employment, women still undertake the
bulk of domestic and childcare duties (see Brannen and Moss, 1988).
As Gittins (1985) has commented, men's participation in domestic
tasks remains largely voluntary, whereas 'if a woman *chooses* not to
keep the house clean, not to supervise the children adequately, she is
in danger of being labelled a "bad" mother and wife.' Just how deep-
rooted are these notions of the woman's role is indicated by the fact

that the questions asked in surveys of domestic life are conventionally framed in terms which ask whether men *help* with the (thereby implicity female) tasks of childcare and housework.

It is fascinating to observe how the new demands of the labour market have produced a striking ambivalence in the official view of the roles and responsibilities of mothers. For decades the argument has been ardently advanced, particularly by the political Right, that mothers of young children who shirk their duty by going out to work place the development of their offspring at risk. In a recent Parliamentary debate on family policy, however, a former Conservative minister, emphasising that it was now in the national interest for women to contribute to the economy, was able to proclaim that 'it's nonsense to suggest that working women cannot be good mothers. That is a ludicrous statement and I reject it out of hand' (*The Guardian*, 16 March 1990).

Such a change of view has not, however, been accompanied by any shift in the policy position which recognises little or no public contribution to enabling mothers to reconcile the competing demands of employment and family life.

The privacy of the family

Before examining the ways in which the notion of the mother's responsibility for children is reflected in the public approach to child care, it is important to look at the other ideological pillar supporting a non-interventionist policy, namely, the perceived privacy of family life. We live in a society which assumes little *collective* responsibility for the shape and fabric of children's lives, especially those under school age, and there is a broad consensus that the internal world of the family is not a legitimate area for public intervention (for example, Henwood and others 1987). As Gittins (op. cit.) notes:

'what actually goes on in the family is conveniently dismissed as "private" until it becomes "public" by creating a nuisance or a financial responsibility for the state.'

It is useful here to distinguish between two very different aspects of social policy and action: one which is concerned to *protect* children from damage and harm, and the other which seeks to *promote* their welfare and development. To the extent that the privacy of family life is a dominant value, public policy is likely to be confined to the former, with little state interference in what parents do with their children except to protect or rescue them from abuse or neglect. As Land and Parker (1978) have pointed out:

'the state has been disinclined to offer services unless a family's ability to care has crumbled or disappeared through death or inadequacy.'

The outcome of this policy stance in Britain is clearly visible in the public provision of day care. Fewer than two per cent of children under five are catered for in local authority day nurseries, and their essentially *protective* function is evidenced by the fact that places are available only to those in defined categories of priority need (see, for example, Van der Eyken, 1984). Except in times of national emergency, these categories have never included working mothers, whose responsibility it has remained to seek private solutions to the problem of day care.

When it comes to ensuring that children enjoy experiences which would actively *promote* their well-being and development, the dominant ideology of the privacy of the family again reasserts itself. Despite the ongoing debate within the child development world as to the precise contribution of different components in various childcare settings, there is a wealth of theoretical and empirical knowledge concerning the importance of the early years for subsequent development, and the conditions conducive to healthy physical, intellectual and emotional growth (see, for example, Phillips, 1987). But there is very little collective concern to ensure that all children do, in fact, enjoy such beneficial circumstances. This is exemplified in the long-standing, yet unfulfilled, commitment to nursery education; a commitment which – since first advocated by the Plowden Report in 1965, and most recently by policy statements of the two main political parties – is expressed in terms of providing nursery schooling for all three and four-year-olds *whose parents wish it*. Thus, where such provision exists, the power of choice lies with parents, and there would be little social censure of those who chose not to avail themselves of the service on behalf of their children.

The topic of nursery education is also of significance in relation to our earlier discussion of family responsibility for childcare. The administrative division in Britain between pre-school education and day care, for so long criticised for its artificiality and divisiveness in terms of children's needs, is deeply rooted in the prevailing ideological view of the boundaries of state and family responsibility. Thus, the policy commitment to the expansion of state nursery *education* – long regarded as a legitimate area for public intervention – contrasts with an explicit refusal to provide for children's day *care*, which is related, as Hoy and Kennedy (1983) suggest, to the fear that the family might abdicate what is seen as its own responsibility for children in favour of state support.

The current response

This ideological view of the rights and responsibilities of the family underpin the governmental response to the newly-recognised need for an expansion of day care facilities. While this now concedes that women *can* successfully combine full time work and competent mothering, it is not seen as the state's business actively to assist them to do so. This is consistent, of course, with the present political goal of encouraging private solutions and restraining public expenditure.

The resulting policy is that, as before, the increase in demand for day care is to be satisfied through the operation of the private market. A major difference in the current scenario, however, is the Government's stated expectation that, since the situation has been created by the economy's need for mothers to work, employers will play a key role in its resolution.

Is this in fact likely to happen? A glance at recent media reports would suggest that the country was witnessing a mushrooming growth of private day care services, in particular employer-provided workplace nurseries. A more considered view of the situation, however, leads one to be more cautious in assessing these developments; first in terms of whether they will actually meet the need on the scale required, and secondly whether, from a child or family-centred standpoint, they represent a desirable solution.

As far as the level of provision is concerned it seems clear that, since it will be dictated primarily by considerations of economic advantage, availability will be highly variable among different sectors of employment and different occupations. A recent survey revealed marked regional variations in workplace nursery provision, with facilities to date confined almost exclusively to the south-east of England (Working for Childcare, 1990). The same report included the following telling comments from the personnel manager of one of the major companies surveyed:

'It would be foolish to be too complacent about the prospects for large scale private sector provision... employers will take a hard-headed commercial viewpoint on whether to go ahead with child care provision and resent being asked to perform a social services type role. Child care policy is still seen by many companies as an "optional extra", to be shelved when more urgent considerations arise.'

It is pertinent to note in this context that, despite the publicity given to new developments, some long-established workplace nurseries in traditional areas of women's employment have actually *closed* in recent years (Cohen, 1988). This emphasises the inadequacy of a market-led solution as far as the interests of families are concerned. The needs of the national economy may have put day care on the public agenda, but it is family income which is relevant to the decision of most women regarding employment. There is little reason to suppose that the relationship between the two would be such as to ensure that the day care needs of all existing or potential employees would be met. It is highly probable that provision will be targeted in order to recruit and retain professional workers, so that those with less marketable skills will not enjoy equality of access.

It is important, also, to consider the implications for children of a day care service based on current economic exigencies, rather than on a concept of social responsibility for family support and childcare. It is difficult to reconcile the notion of high quality provision with what is the care equivalent of a tied cottage. As Moss (1990) has pointed out, the stability of care is dependent upon the parent remaining in the same employment; it weakens the family's links with its local community and may, especially in large urban centres, involve children in an undesirable amount of travelling. Recent experience in the United States may also invoke a cautionary approach to such developments in this country. Workplace day care has proved unpopular with parents, who prefer provision in their home locality. On the employers' side, it has been found to be expensive, under-used and administratively cumbersome, with the result that only 35,000 out of six million employers are estimated to be providing such facilities (Clarke Stewart, 1990).

From a child-centred viewpoint, therefore, it may be felt that the improbability of a massive expansion of workplace nursery provision is not to be wholly regretted. What, however, is likely to be the alternative? As far as employer' support for childcare is concerned, a simultaneous development is the provision of an *indirect* contribution in the form of childcare vouchers. This has the attraction for employers of putting back on to parents the onus of actually finding suitable care. And for the majority of parents, this is likely to mean turning to what has always been the main source of out-of-home day care in Britain: the private childminder.

Childminding: the preferred solution

The legislative history of childminding is thus one of minimal state involvement in what has nonetheless been officially endorsed as a private market response to the increasing demand for day care. Indeed, childminding has been regarded by successive governments as their preferred solution to the childcare problems of working parents. In the light of the arguments put forward earlier, it is not difficult to see why this should be so. From the ever-dominant economic standpoint, it makes little demand on the public purse. At the Sunningdale Conference, which took place in 1976 with the aim of seeking low-cost solutions to the already evident problem of inadequate day care, most participants came out in favour of an expansion of childminding. As a service, it was claimed, it required no expensive buildings, equipment or – of particular interest to our present study – training for its practitioners (DHSS, 1976). Such comments suggest that childminder training, if it was considered necessary at all, would be limited in scope by comparison with that of other childcare workers.

It has already been noted that, as an essentially private activity, childminding is consistent with a view of the family, specifically the mother, as responsible for childcare. But there is a further ideological dimension which becomes significant here. Although we have suggested that, in this area, public policy in Britain is not driven by child-centred considerations, this is not to say that it lacks a rationalising view of what is good for children; in particular, a view which fits in with that of the mother as the key figure in the care of children. The child-based perspective which supports a policy of minimal state involvement in the provision of day care goes back to the post-war period and, in particular, the work of John Bowlby (1952). His theory of maternal deprivation and the need for continuous care by a stable adult offered a child-centred justification for the acceptance of childminding, rather than nursery provision, as the solution to the day care requirements of working parents.

Thus, childminding has been strongly endorsed in official circles as more appropriate than group care for meeting *children's* needs, especially those in the younger half of the pre-school age range.

'From the child's point of view, a good minder can provide him (*sic*) with informal care in familiar surroundings that is the nearest substitute to his own home, and also give him the opportunity to form the close, continuing relationships which much research has shown to be important for his development; for many children under three and those with special problems this is much more in tune with their limited capacity for social contacts than the communal experience of a day nursery.' (Joint letter issued by DHSS and DES, 1978)

Outside official circles, however, the proclaimed advantages of childminding have been widely challenged. Numerous writers have pointed out that, in financial terms, it is a low cost solution only in terms of *public* expenditure; that the real costs are borne both by parents, who may be charged a substantial proportion of their earnings, and by childminders, to whom the fees may nonetheless represent a derisory level of pay (for example, Challis, 1981; Hoy and Kennedy, 1983). As far as the quality of provision is concerned, it has been cogently argued that a service subject to weak legislative control, and under-resourced in terms of supervision and support, is not amenable to the setting and implementation of high standards of care (Tizard and others, 1976). Furthermore, surveys of the consumer view have consistently indicated a parental preference for nursery provision (see, for example, Bone, 1977).

Despite these wide-ranging reservations, it does seem clear that, for the reasons outlined earlier, childminding is likely to continue in its role as the major source of day care for children of working parents. Studies of the arrangements made for childcare have shown that, while relatives remain the most common providers, childminding is by far the most widely used form of care outside the home. The 1981 Women in Employment survey revealed that approximately one in five working mothers with pre-school children used the services of a childminder (Martin and Roberts, 1984). It was noted earlier that the admission policies of local authority day nurseries made this form of provision inaccessible to most working parents. Recent estimates of the number of places offered by *private* nurseries indicate that these, too, represent only a fraction of the provision available from registered childminders (Melhuish and Moss, 1991). Although it is impossible to gauge with any accuracy the number of unregistered providers who are offering a day care service, recent authoritative estimates suggest that their number is in the region of 20 per cent of the figure for registered minders (Moss, 1987).

Official statistics also indicate that, well in advance of the currently acknowledged day care crisis, the continuing rise in rates of maternal employment was being accompanied by a steady increase in the supply of childminders. For example, in the decade between 1976 and 1986, the number of registered minders more than doubled, rising from 31,000 to 64,000 (DHSS, 1976; DHSS, 1986).

Thus, childminding seems likely to continue as the answer to the day care needs of most working parents. As such, it is important to discover more about how childminding operates and how it is changing. What kind of service is it that appears to hover uncertainly between the domains of public sector regulation and the private world of family life? The general thrust of the pressure for change in childminding in this country has been directed at the status of childminders as workers and at the standards of the service which they provide. That this is taking place within a legislative and policy framework which postulates minimal public intervention in the actual operation of the service, points to a situation in which contradiction and ambiguity are inherent. This is especially evident in relation to what we have suggested is potentially the most radical strategy for change: namely, the introduction of training for childminding.

The earlier account of the legislation governing the registration of childminders showed that there is no specific requirement that those wishing to pursue this activity should possess any qualification relevant to working with young children or have had any appropriate experience. However, the concept of training for childminding has been enthusiastically espoused at a number of levels over the past 20 years or so, ranging from the ministerial circulars urging local authorities to develop support services for childminders, to the activist organisations of practitioners themselves. At the practical level, an increasing number of local authorities have introduced courses for childminders, either before or after registration, and the National Childminding Association has itself been involved, in conjunction with the Open University, in the production of a training pack (OU/NCMA, 1986).

But what exactly is meant by training for childminding? How is this notion accommodated within a service which, as we have seen, operates with one foot in the public domain and the other in the world of unregulated private enterprise? Above all, perhaps, what impact does the experience of training have on how childminders conduct their activities and on how well childminding arrangements work? It was questions such as these which led us to focus on training, in particular, in our study of childminding and how childminding arrangements operate. In the next chapter, we look more closely at the concept of training in relation to this type of day care, at the issues which it raises, and at how the study was approached.

2. Issues in childminder training

Training is fundamentally about producing *change* in the knowledge, skills, awareness or behaviour of its recipients. In contrast to education, with its literal concern to 'lead out' and develop the individual in a broad sense, training has the narrower purpose of preparing and equipping people to undertake specific tasks and responsibilities. Its content is thus inherently bound up with subsequent application or performance in a defined role or activity. In the occupational sphere, training is conventionally employed as a principal strategy for change, whether in relation to aspirant or to established workers. For the former, its broad goal is to equip would-be practitioners to fulfil the requirements of a particular work role – indeed, training often performs a regulatory function by restricting access to those who have thereby demonstrated their competence. For those already involved, in-service training may seek to enhance their existing performance, or enable them to adapt to changes and developments in their occupational environment.

With this view of training in mind, it would be tempting to interpret its recent emergence in the field of childminding as an indication that those who care for young children in this way are moving out of the twilight world of domestic labour and into the area of publicly-recognised and regulated occupational activity. But, in the light of our foregoing discussion of the past and present framework within which childminding is conducted, this would be a somewhat simplistic assumption. Indeed, when we begin to pose questions about why and how the issue of training has been introduced into the childminding scene, a number of paradoxes and ambiguities emerge, which point to its complexity as a topic for research.

As indicated in the preceding chapter, the stimulus for the development of training for childminders has come from two main sources – the relevant authorities at central and local government level, and organised representatives of childminders themselves. In both cases, although with varying emphasis, the impetus has stemmed from disquiet over certain perceived deficiencies of childminding in terms of the standards of provision and the status of providers. However, the adoption of training as a remedial strategy would seem to present a number of problems on both counts; problems which derive from the policy framework within which childminding operates and the way in which the activity itself is perceived.

Standards and the official approach to training

Central government recommendations in this area have, from the beginning, implicitly hinged on considerations of the quality of care received by minded children. As long ago as 1965, passing reference was made to the notion of training for childminders in a ministerial circular which, like the original legislation governing childminding, was largely concerned with standards of provision in day nurseries:

'(The local authority) will wish to ensure that those in charge of the nursery or those minding children have some knowledge of the special needs of children. Where they have had no formal training, the authority's staff can assist by giving individual instruction or by inviting them to spend some time in a day nursery, nursery school or nursery class.' (Ministry of Health Circular 5/65)

No indication was given, however, of what the scope or content of such 'training' should be, or of how it was to be resourced and delivered. A few years later, a further circular took up the point again, but shed no more light on the perceived nature and purpose of training. Indeed, the vagueness of the document was matched only by its pomposity. Referring to 'persons without professional qualifications...engaged in childminding' it noted that:

'These will frequently be housewives whose experience will be limited to bringing up their own children, which may often be insufficient to equip a woman to look after other people's children. Many such women will have had the advantages of general instruction in child care from a health visitor...For this group it might be appropriate to organise...short courses at clinics or in nursery premises.' (Ministry of Health Circular 37/68)

Ten years on, a Local Authority Social Services Letter (LASSL(78)), on the topic of coordination of services for under-fives, invited authorities to 'review their support and advice services, including in-service training, for childminders'. It also urged the fostering of links between childminders and other pre-school services such as nursery schools and playgroups, in order to broaden the experience of children who, being 'merely minded' (*sic*), were 'more likely than other children to be denied the social and intellectual stimulation that is important to their development'.

We shall look more closely in a later chapter at what is actually known about the experience and development of children cared for by childminders. Here, however, it is sufficient to note that the rather negative and disparaging view of childminding which permeates these official documents was reinforced by a number of studies in the late 1960s and 1970s, which were critical of the care provided by substantial proportions of childminders (for example, Bryant and others, 1980; Jackson and Jackson, 1979; Mayall and Petrie, 1977; 1983). It also seems probable that official unease about standards was fuelled by the fact that what was, quantitatively at least, the most important day care service was, by its very nature, virtually invisible and inaccessible to public scrutiny.

Whatever the underlying motives for official advocacy of child-minder training, central government pronouncements on the subject, as exemplified above, have been characterised by the modesty of its envisaged scope, an implicit assumption of voluntary take-up and a certain vagueness of objectives. All three features are, however, inextricably linked to an overall policy position which offers little ideological support for vigorous, committed intervention. The prevailing view of childminding as an essentially *private* activity involving minimal state expenditure, is hardly compatible with an ambitious approach to training necessitating large-scale public investment.

The limited scope of childminder training as envisaged by central government – in comparison to that undertaken by others working with young children such as teachers and nursery nurses – is exemplified by the references to short courses, nursery visits and discussion groups in the official documents quoted above. This is clearly in tune with the preference for childminding as a low-cost solution to the problem of inadequate day care – at least in terms of public expenditure and involvement (see, for example, ACC/AMA, 1977; DHSS, 1976).

The view that the experience of training should be dependent upon voluntary take-up by childminders is also consistent with a policy stance which sees their activities as essentially private. This position has not gone unchallenged however: a TUC Working Party on the Under Fives stated that:

'it would, in our view, be illogical to suppose that, while all under fives workers – nursery nurses, nursery leaders, playgroup workers – need training, the same is not true for childminders.' (TUC, 1979)

Furthermore, an approach to training which relies entirely on the motivation of practitioners to seek self-improvement has been criticised as being based on the questionable assumption that childminders will perceive themselves as deficient caregivers and thus in need of change (Bryant and others, 1980; Mayall and Petrie, 1983).

As far as the actual objectives of training are concerned, a particular problem lies in identifying the specific requirements for a role which, as we have noted, has been endorsed for its approximation to mothering. A further, related dilemma for a training agenda which seeks to address standards in the context of a private activity, is presented by the diversity of values among different individuals, families and groups in our multiracial, multicultural society. Whose beliefs, standards and practices are to count, and in what circumstances, are questions of both theoretical and empirical importance for a service which operates without a coherent public value base. At the governmental level, however, the predicament in which this places the notion of training has been given insufficient recognition. Neither the controlling legislation nor the official circulars and guidance documents consider the question of quality or standards in childminding in a way that would indicate what training should be for, what it should consist of, and what trained childminders should do.

It is worth noting, however, perhaps, that Britain is by no means unique in this respect. The United States, for example, also has a non-interventionist policy towards day care, and, as Deller (1989) writes:

'there exists no consensus among caregivers, state and local officials, child development experts, researchers or federal legislators or administrators on what would constitute an effective and workable uniform set of standards for child care in this country.'

Other training issues

Standards of childcare and the quality of provision for children are obviously central to the question of childminder training. However, the initiatives which have come from the grassroots movement, and, as we shall see, from local authority workers directly involved in the design and delivery of courses, explicitly take a broader view of what childminding involves and the issues which training might address.

Although childminding has been viewed, albeit not unanimously, as an extension of mothering in relation to the children cared for, it is clear that there are important aspects of the childminder's role which involve quite different tasks and behaviour. These are very much the product of the essentially private context in which childminding currently operates, and include the organisational abilities required to run a business single-handed, plus the interpersonal skills needed to conduct a one-to-one relationship with other adults – in particular the parents of minded children. This is, of course, a potentially difficult and sensitive relationship, made all the more so by the lack of a supportive framework of socially accepted rules of behaviour.

It is a recognition of the wide-ranging and often challenging nature of the tasks involved in childminding which has led many of its champions to bemoan the low status attached to the work and to advocate training for childminders as a strategy for amelioration (for example, Beckwith, 1982). However, there is no simple, direct relationship between training and status in the occupational world in general, and a reflection upon the position of childminding in our society suggests that it would be over-optimistic to see training in itself as the key to a new, improved image.

It is important here to consider childminding as one of many forms of work with children, since the criteria by which it is socially valued – or otherwise – are more widely applicable. The status and rewards attached to such work vary according to a number of inter-linked factors, including the diffuseness or specialism of the task, the age of the children concerned, and the gender of the worker. Within the field of education, for example, lower status tends to be awarded to work which is seen to require comparatively little expertise, which involves children in the younger age groups and which is generally undertaken by women (Musgrave, 1972). The image of childmind-ing, which would suffer on all three counts, is further depressed by its association with mothering and the domestic, caring role of women – one which is perceived as 'natural' or 'instinctive', and hence unspecialised and unworthy of reward. Gittins (1985) draws attention to the artificial division which has arisen since the period of industrialisation between the status attaching to paid work *outside* the home and the corresponding degradation of unpaid domestic labour. It is interesting to draw a parallel between the low status of childminding and that of, for example, residential workers, whose role as described in the Wagner Report (1988) was also equated with domestic and family commitments – 'the assumption being that such duties are unskilled and undemanding responsibilities'. Finally, it is important to consider how status attaches to childminding as a form of *day care*. In its public form in our society, day care is often seen as stigmatised by virtue of being reserved for inadequate, 'failing' families; while in its private capacity, including childminding, it is widely perceived to represent the abrogation of parental – especially maternal – responsibility. In the light of all these considerations, the introduction of modest training initiatives would appear to be a somewhat frail weapon with which to attack the low status from which childminding continues to suffer.

Research on training

It will already be clear that the issue of training for childminding is a complex one, and that an empirical enquiry cannot adequately address its impact without taking into account the context in which childminding takes place and the perspectives of the main parties involved. Before describing how the present study was undertaken, however, it is important to look briefly at what we know from our own earlier work in this field and from other research on the topic of training.

Our previous investigation involved interviewing a random sam-ple of 200 registered childminders in order to explore their responses to a wide range of support services, including their views and actual experience of childminder training (Ferri and Birchall, 1987). This revealed that a majority of those interviewed had either attended some kind of relevant course or expressed an interest in doing so. It was interesting to discover that the actual take-up of training, or positive attitudes to the notion, were not related in any way to the childminders' personal backgrounds in terms of age, social class or educational level. Nor was there any apparent link with factors in their childminding experience, such as the length of time they had been involved or expected to continue, or their reasons for embarking upon it in the first place.

At first sight, such findings might appear to be a positive indication of the broad-based appeal of training initiatives. However, since they run counter to the long-established associations between social and educational background and response to training in the traditional sphere of occupations, a more cautious interpretation seems to be called for. Our data also suggested that much of the satisfaction expressed by childminders in relation to course attendance derived from the peer group support and contact which it had offered. It seemed particularly important, therefore, to examine more deeply how childminder training is perceived by its potential recipients, and to look at how these perceptions match the aims and objectives of those advocating and delivering such provision.

As far as the precise influence of training is concerned, very little conclusive evidence emerges from the two broad types of investigation which have been undertaken to date. The first group includes a number of quantitative studies, mostly carried out in the United States, which have indicated that caregiver training is one of several factors associated with positive child development outcomes in a variety of pre-school settings, including family day care or childminding (for example, Belsky, 1980; Clarke-Stewart, 1987; Goelman and Pence, 1987; Philips and Howes, 1987; Ruopp and others, 1979). However, for a number of reasons, such findings do not go far to advance our understanding in a way that holds clear policy implications for the development of training. First, the differences are not consistent; partly, no doubt, because they deal with a range of different developmental outcomes and different care environments. More importantly perhaps, from the standpoint of policy and practice, the findings merely point to a positive relationship between training and the indicators concerned, rather than direct causal links. Training tends to be treated as a global variable; there is little or no exploration of what it consists of, how it is translated into practice and, of particular importance, the dynamic relationship between specific aspects of training and the measures being examined. It should also be noted that, as far as childminding is concerned, concentration on child development outcomes seriously neglects a number of adult-related questions which are particularly important in this type of day care, and which have been addressed in some depth in the present study.

The second group of relevant studies, of which a number have been carried out in Britain, focuses more specifically on the content of training, and the response of its recipients, in a variety of pre-school settings. Here, however, the research data, although useful, tend to be more subjective in nature. Estimates of the impact of training rely heavily on consumer self-assessment, and highlight the difficulty of evaluation in this area. Thus, the investigations of the development of training programmes relating to the High/Scope Pre-School Curriculum shows a high level of trainee satisfaction with the experience, but little independent, objective evidence of a measured impact on subsequent work performance (Sylva and others, 1986). In our own earlier work in the area of childminding, we found that among those who had had the experience of training, only about a quarter felt that their views or practice had changed in any way as a result (Ferri and Birchall, 1987). Similar findings emerged from another National Children's Bureau study, which evaluated an innovatory childminding support scheme, operated by the National Childminding Association, and which included the provision of training courses. The opinions of the support scheme workers were that childminders who had attended courses had enjoyed and valued the experience, but they were less convinced that significant changes had taken place in their approach to their work (Ferri and Stern, 1987).

The methodological complexity of evaluating the impact of training in terms of change in behaviour and values has been commented on in other spheres, particularly those in which its development is at an embryonic stage. Berridge and others (1985) point to the need in such cases to be wary in interpreting even the 'soft' data of consumer-based responses:

'The fact that the majority find the training experience highly satisfactory should also be received with caution. Those that seek training are already predisposed to welcome the experience and, rather like the celibate, previously having had nothing leads one keenly to appreciate even the most modest stimulation.'

In the area of childminding, only Jackson's (1979) modest study of one particular training programme offered some objective measure of impact, and the findings revealed little or no significant difference in subsequent practice. It is important to note that this result is in line with others in different fields which have studied training as an effective strategy for long-term change. Thus, for example, a review of the efficacy of teacher training concluded that:

'almost every relevant investigation, whatever the instrument used, has found that changes in expressed attitudes during training are followed by changes in the opposite direction during the first year of teaching.' (Morrison and McIntyre, 1969)

The above point underlines the importance of studying the *context* in which particular kinds of work take place and at how training relates to this. Georgiades and Phillimore (1975), for example, have challenged the assumption that directing training at individuals will bring about organisational change. This has an important message for the application of training to childminding, and the implicit view that it will be influential in raising both the standards and status of practitioners. As Katz and Kahn (1966) claim, this approach rests upon:

'the psychological fallacy of concentrating upon individuals without regard to the role relationships that constitute the social system of which they are a part.'

Similar views have been advanced in the field of day care itself. Powell (1982), for example, argues that evaluative research needs to look beyond the narrow confines of child-based outcomes to the social and occupational worlds of which day care is a part:

'The compatibility of two or more social systems (ie, family, day care setting) depends on the nature of the relations between key members of those social systems.'

It was considerations such as these which made it clear that the impact of childminder training could not be properly studied within the narrow boundaries of one or more specific courses. Instead, the role and development of such training had to be viewed within a broader context, which included both the private and public worlds – of minders, parents and local authority workers – in which this particular form of day care takes place. The theoretical framework which was adopted for the study, and the methods by which it was carried out, are described in full in the following chapter.

3. How the study was carried out

As the previous chapter has indicated, the activity of childminding brings together a number of separate but interrelated contexts: in the private domain these include the domestic and occupational circumstances of the family seeking day care; and the corresponding situation of the childminder who provides it. In the public sphere they consist of the relevant policies and practices within the local authority departments responsible for overseeing childminding, as well as the wider political, economic and ideological frameworks within which all of the foregoing are embedded.

Theoretical framework of the study

Thus, in order to carry out an evaluative study of the part played by training in this type of day care, it was considered important to look at how childminding operates *within* these various contexts and in terms of the links *between* them. The conceptual framework adopted for the research was derived from the ecological approach developed by Bronfenbrenner (1977). Briefly, this involves an analysis of the relationships between different levels of the environment surrounding, in this case, the individual child. In the area of childminding, this includes the links between home and day care settings; between both of these and the social services structures relating to childminding (of which training initiatives are part); and, encompassing all of these, the economic, political and ideological factors which impinge upon the provision and use of day care. In terms of the criteria by which to judge the quality of the service examined in this way, it was thus necessary to extend the area of enquiry beyond the conventional confines of child development indicators to include aspects of childminding arrangements which were of significance to parents and minders themselves. This is not to say that child-based outcomes were ignored or awarded less importance; but rather to emphasise that, in identifying these (described in more detail in Chapter 8), account was taken of the perspectives of the key adult actors in the childminding situation – parents, minders and local authority workers – in addition to our own explicit views derived from theory and research.

While parental involvement has been widely investigated in studies of early childhood education and institutional day care – albeit usually as instrumental to the achievement of child-centred goals – the parental perspective in childminding has received much less attention. The comparative neglect of the adult perspective in much research in this field is a serious shortcoming when it is remembered that for neither parents nor childminders are child-centred motives likely to be the sole, or even the prime, reason for seeking or providing day care.

For parents, issues of affordability, accessibility, reliability and flexibility are likely to be of importance in finding satisfactory day care, in addition to their wishes regarding the experience to be provided for their children. Furthermore, as other writers (for example, Belsky, 1980; Powell 1982) have noted, there has been very little investigation of potentially positive *adult* outcomes in day care arrangements, in terms of, for example, enlarged social networks, personal friendships or new ideas and insights regarding child-rearing.

Neither has the critical area of the relationships between child-minder and parent received much in-depth examination. As Moss (1987) has pointed out, studies which have considered the adult relationships involved in childminding, have tended to document each side's negative assessments of the other, without probing further into how problems arise and, importantly in terms of outcomes, if and how they are resolved.

A particularly significant issue here is the *power* relationship between childminder and parent. In other service settings, impor-tant changes have taken place in recent years in the direction of greater empowerment of parents (for example, Ferri and Saunders, 1991; Pugh and De'ath 1989), changes which have been given a formal legislative framework by the 1989 Children Act. This shift has represented a challenging, often discomforting, experience for parents and professionals alike. However, it also involves a move away from an earlier position in which the role boundaries between providers and users of children's services were more clearly defined and separated. In childminding, the situation is very different. We know little of the power relationship between parents and child-minders, or of the factors which are of significance to it, such as age, social background and childcare experience, for example. Clearly, however, this issue is likely to be of central importance to how a day care arrangement works and to the role of training in childminding.

Our earlier discussion of the conflicting ideologies concerning women as mothers and as workers also raises important questions about the relationship between providers and users of childminding services. How do these ideologies influence mothers' and minders' perceptions of their respective roles in this day care setting, in which the minder is enacting a caring, home-based role in relation to the child of another parent who has chosen to do something else? How, in turn, does this affect the triangular relationship between minder, parent and child, and how the day care arrangement is negotiated and conducted? The location of *power* in this context, and how it operates in respect of factors such as supply and demand in day care provision, the terms and conditions of the arrangement, and the nature of the actual provision for children, remains virtually unexplored territory – yet it is crucial to our understanding of how childminding works and the potential for intervention.

The need for a qualitative approach

The complexity of the issues involved in a study such as this also pointed to the need for a methodology which would generate a body of rich, qualitative information. Instead of undertaking a large-scale, statistical approach which would seek out quantitative relationships among a broad set of categorised variables, we wanted to obtain a more subtle understanding of what childminding entailed for those involved, and what, for them, were the significant factors which contributed to the success or otherwise of a particular day care arrangement.

Such an approach was considered essential, not only for under-standing the operation of childminding in general, but especially for assessing the actual or potential contribution of training to this kaleidoscopic form of day care. As noted earlier, much of the previous research in this area has looked simply at the relationship between particular child-based outcomes and whether or not care providers have received training of some kind. The limitations of such an approach have been summed up by Powell's (1982) observation that it 'reduces intensive human service programmes to a set of causal relationships'. In contrast, a qualitative methodology focuses attention on *how* things work rather than *whether* they work, and, in so doing, seeks a detailed understanding of the perspectives which various participants bring to the situation under investigation (Howe, 1988, Taylor and Bogdan, 1984). Moreover, the application of the ecological framework referred to above required in-depth information relating to the different contexts which are brought together by the activity of childminding. It was essential, therefore, to collect detailed data relating to the circumstances, attitudes and behaviour of both the users and providers of this type of day care. Only thus could we fully explore and evaluate the contribution of training to how childminding is conducted.

The study

With these considerations in mind, the method chosen for the research was a case study approach, in which 'cases' were represented by childminding *arrangements*. Each case, therefore, included minder, parent and child. A unique and important feature of the research design was that each sample case should consist of a *new* placement, so that key issues regarding the wishes and expectations of both parties, the negotiation and actual start of the arrangement could be explored at the earliest possible point.

The two-and-a-half year project began towards the end of 1987. The fieldwork was carried out in two local authority areas, the Bracknell Division of Berkshire and part of the London Borough of Waltham Forest. The first is in a county authority comprising a new town and surrounding smaller towns and villages, whose socio-economic characteristics make it typical of the relatively affluent south-east of England. The selected division of Waltham Forest, on the other hand, is an inner city area with a substantial minority ethnic population and a considerable degree of social and economic disadvantage. The two areas were deliberately chosen for their environmental contrasts, as well as for their well-established, although differing, approaches to childminder training.

The first stage of the work involved collecting detailed information of policy and practice regarding childminding, including training, in each area. This was obtained by means of semi-structured interviews with social services staff at various levels, from those with day-to-day responsibility for the childminding service through to Assistant Director. The researchers then attended training courses for prospective childminders in each area as observers, to obtain a first-hand picture of how the described objectives were translated into practice, and to see how they were received by participants. In addition, it helped to focus on a number of key issues which could be explored further in the subsequent case studies of childminding in operation.

Sample of childminding arrangements

The social services workers in each area provided a list of registered minders, including details of their date of registration, attendance at courses, or use of other support facilities and, in the one area which recorded such information, the minders' racial background. Letters were sent from the research team to every minder on the lists, telling them of the research and asking them to inform us of any new children placed with them in the coming months.

From just over 200 new arrangements reported to us over a period of a year or so, we selected 15 in each area for our target case study sample of 30. In choosing cases, we were careful to ensure that a range of situations and user/provider characteristics were represented. For example, it was important to have a sample of childminders with varying amounts of minding experience and, while we were particularly interested in those who had attended training courses, we also deliberately included a small number (eight out of the 30) who had not. As far as minded children were concerned, although the sample was confined to those below school age, it was selected to include an age range from young babies to children of three and over. As the number of cases accrued, the social class and racial background of both provider and user families were carefully monitored to ensure that a variety of participants were represented. Since, as we explain below, this was to be a follow-up study, a further criterion for selection was that the arrangement was, at the outset, expected by both parties to be of long-term duration.

It should be stressed that *range* rather than *representativeness* of sample characteristics was considered crucial for an in-depth, qualitative study such as this. To seek a representative sample, in terms of user or provider characteristics, would have been neither feasible nor relevant. It should also be noted that the acquisition of the sample was a long and laborious process. The figure of 30 selected cases is but a fraction of those approached and discarded for a variety of reasons, including refusal to take part, or unsuitability in terms of one or more of the relevant factors indicated above.

Interviews

Childminders and parents in the 30 selected cases were contacted by letter and invited to take part in the study. The main method of data collection involved two semi-structured interviews with each participant, carried out in their own homes. Among the parental group, fathers as well as mothers were interviewed wherever possible, since it was considered important to try to counter the general neglect of the paternal role in day care research. Ideally, childminders' husbands or partners would also have been included; however, since the interviews with parents, and attendance at training courses, already necessitated a substantial amount of evening work, it was not possible to add to this by carrying out further evening interviews in the childminders' homes.

The first interview took place as soon as possible after the new day care arrangement began. The topics were wide-ranging; parents were asked why they had sought day care, what types they had considered, what was important to them in finding provision, and how they had contacted and chosen their childminder. In talking to the providers, the focus was on their reason for childminding, how the work fitted in with their other activities and responsibilities, their perception of the childminder's role, and the structure within which they operated. Both parties were asked to give their accounts of the terms and conditions of the arrangement, how these had been negotiated and agreed, and the early stages of introducing and settling the child. Of particular interest at the time of this first interview was how the training provided for childminders in each area had addressed the vital issue of negotiating and establishing new day care arrangements. It is important to emphasise that in this, as in the subsequent aspects investigated, our approach to the analysis of childminder training was an interactive one. Thus, we were looking not only for indicators of the impact of any courses attended, but also for implications for the development of training arising out of our examination of what actually took place in the conduct of the case study arrangements.

The second interview, approximately 10 months later, was designed to obtain a detailed picture of how the arrangement was working from the perspective of all those involved. By the time of this follow-up, 15 of the 30 arrangements had been terminated. This in itself is an important finding, and the circumstances surrounding the ending of placements are discussed in Chapter 9. Except for three childminders and three parents, however, all the participants were re-interviewed.

The second interview obtained detailed descriptions of the day-to-day provision for the minded children, and the contact and communication between the adults involved; the relationships which had developed between minders, parents and children; and each party's accounts of their respective beliefs and practices in matters of childcare, and how any areas of disagreement, either explicit or implicit, were dealt with. The nature of the experiences provided for minded children, and the relationships between caregivers and children, are key aspects of the day care situation, so it was important to obtain detailed information on these topics also, in order to explore the actual and potential role of training in promoting satisfactory outcomes.

Observations

The researchers also carried out periods of observation in the childminding setting, shortly after the second interview had taken place. This provided another important source of data pertaining to the experience of the minded children in the sample. It furnished an independent assessment of how far the quality of provision reflected the standards articulated by the parents and childminders involved, by those responsible for training in each area, and the criteria which we, as researchers, brought to the study from the literature on child development. Full details of how the observations were conducted are contained in Chapter 8.

Analysis

The raw data of qualitative research consists, as in this study, of lengthy scripts of transcribed interviews and detailed narrative records of observed activity and interaction. Such material, unlike its quantitative equivalent, does not lend itself to even the simplest form of tabulation or numerical comparison. However, the approach to the analysis of qualitative data must be no less systematic and rigorous. The technique employed for this study was based on those adopted by other qualitative researchers in work aimed, like ours, at developing an in-depth understanding of the settings and people under study (for example, Quinn Patton, 1980; Taylor and Bogdan, 1984).

Briefly, this first involved scrutinising the data for the emergence of key, recurring themes which appeared to be of importance for the childminding arrangement. One theme, for example, which appears at the very beginning of an arrangement is the economic aspect of day care and, in particular, the charge for childminding. The significance this has for minders and parents, however, and how it relates to other factors in their lives, may be very different. Also, this significance may vary *among* minders and *among* parents according to their differing circumstances and experiences.

The next stage of analysis, therefore, involved looking for patterns and relationships between the themes and other features contained *within* each respondent's account and *between* those of the minder and parent involved in each arrangement. We were especially interested to identify areas of *consensus* or *conflict* in the perspectives brought to the arrangement by the adults concerned. In addition, however, we wanted to examine the interrelationship between this, the private sphere of childminding, and the structural framework which represented its public domain. This was particularly important when it came to comparing the training agenda set by those responsible for its delivery with the reality of the childminding situation in which its messages were to be applied.

In the next chapter, we describe how childminder training was actually approached in our study areas. Also, it is important to look at the broader, public context of childminding as it was represented in the two local authorities, in terms of the structural framework within which it operated, and, in particular, the nature and level of involvement by their social services departments.

4. Training in the two local authorities

As we have already seen, the national policy framework, in terms of legislation and central government guidelines, provides only a skeletal structure within which local social services departments exercise day-to-day responsibility for childminding. In common with most other pre-school provision, childminding is a non-statutory service and is thus highly vulnerable to local political influences and to pressure on scarce resources. As a result, there is enormous variation from one area to another in terms of the priority given to childminding, and day care generally, and the resources allocated in terms of staffing and support services. This variation is also reflected in the approach to childminder training (Ferri and Birchall, 1984; 1987a).

In addition to making training opportunities available, a small number of local authorities have taken a more forceful, intervention-ist approach to the empowering element in the legislation, and adopted a policy of *requiring* prospective childminders to undergo some form of training. This was the case in the two authorities involved in the study, which were deliberately selected for their established policy and practice in this field. There were a number of contrasts, however, in their respective approaches to training, as there were in the socio-economic characteristics of the two areas and in other aspects of the local authority framework surrounding childminding. The following pages present a broad picture of each social services department's overall involvement in childminding, and a more detailed account of its initiatives in the field of training. Information for this part of the study was obtained by interviewing workers with day-to-day responsibility for childminding in each area, as well as those in relevant managerial posts. In addition, the researchers acquired direct insight of the training provision in both localities by observing all sessions of the courses currently in operation.

Bracknell

One of the two areas chosen for the study was the Bracknell division of Berkshire. The social services department was situated in the expanding new town of Bracknell and its catchment area included a number of relatively affluent small towns and villages in the surrounding semi-rural districts. Bracknell itself, with a population of about 100,000, contained two thriving industrial estates and a number of residential areas which planners had hoped would develop as village communities; an aspiration which had not been wholly fulfilled. Provision for under-fives in the division was limited; there were no local authority day nurseries and just one small private day nursery in Bracknell itself. There were four nursery classes attached to infant schools and approximately 1,000 places available in playgroups. For working parents, however, childminders were virtually the only source of day care; at the time the study began there were upwards of 300 registered with the social services department.

Policy and practice

The four part-time day care advisers in the department spent the bulk of their time on childminding, and the remainder on playgroups. All four came from child-centred backgrounds in terms of their initial training (National Nursery Examination Board qualifications) and previous experience, which included work in nursery schools, special schools, day nurseries and playgroups.

When the study began, the departmental structure surrounding the day care advisers and their childminding work was in a state of transition. The Divisional Director post was vacant and this, plus other senior management positions, were temporarily filled by staff in the adjacent tier. As a result, the day care advisers were being supervised by the acting Assistant Divisional Director (Children and Families), in the absence of a suitably experienced Principal Social Worker. According to the acting ADD, childminding *should* have come under the wing of the Principal Officer responsible for the Adoption and Fostering section. This arrangement was not, however, considered appropriate by the day care advisers, who viewed childminding in general as a mainstream form of provision, rather than one for families in difficulties or with special needs.

It was suggested earlier that placing childminding under the auspices of social services departments itself establishes an implicit association with welfare provision. Furthermore, however, the structural location of childminding *within* a social services department gives an important indication of the way in which the activity is perceived. Two points emerge in relation to the situation in Bracknell, which, it should be noted, is by no means unique. First, linking childminding with adoption and fostering brings day care firmly into the sphere of social work and child welfare. At the managerial level in Bracknell, it appeared that this was viewed as the most valid area for departmental intervention in childminding. As the acting Assistant Divisional Director put it:

'From the social services angle, it's the *problem* children that we have difficulty with – we'd like to develop the service more for where a child has problems.'

Such potential development was expressed in terms of the trend referred to in Chapter 1, towards recruiting more childminders specifically to provide for children in the officially defined categories of priority need. At the time of our study, Bracknell employed one salaried childminder with whom it would place such children. There were no other financial resources available for the social services department to subsidise childminding fees; the only way in which such payment could be made was to prevent children coming into care and this could only be done in cases of social, not financial, need.

Apart from this perceived desirability of developing childminding as a *welfare* service, the department's general approach to the activity, at least at senior management level, appeared to be largely non-interventionist: 'We tend to see childminding as a fairly natural thing that happens in the community'. This stance is likely to be linked to the second point to be noted in relation to the place which childminding occupied in the range of social services tasks. In the Bracknell division, the Assistant Divisional Director with managerial responsibility for childminding was also the divisional coordinator for child abuse and the reviewing officer for children in residential care. It is not difficult to appreciate, therefore, that (in his own words) 'Childminding is not mainstream to my knowledge or priorities ... the under fives section don't produce a lot of problems'.

The outcome of the situation appeared to be that a considerable amount of authority and freedom had been granted to the day care advisers (especially the acting senior who had been in post for a number of years) in developing the training programme and other support services for childminders.

Bracknell Children's Centre

In addition to the work of the social services department described above, a leading role in the Bracknell childminding service was played by a national voluntary agency. National Children's Home had, some 15 years previously, set up the Bracknell Children's Centre, which included a childminding project, offering organised play activities for childminders and the children in their care, and run by staff experienced in children's play. The centre had also played a major part in the development of childminder training in Bracknell. In response to requests from local minders eager to raise the standards and public image of childminding, short courses had been introduced at the centre, planned jointly by the unit, the social services day care advisers, and a group of enthusiastic childminders. Over a number of years this course had been developed into a preparatory programme for would-be childminders, which formed the basis of the training strategy in Bracknell at the time of our study.

Training: aims and approaches

A prospective childminder's first encounter with the training provision in Bracknell would be a pre-registration meeting. This was an hour-long lunchtime session held fortnightly in the NCH Children's Centre and led by the head of the centre, a day care adviser and an experienced local childminder. A small group of applicants for registration would be invited (five attended the meeting we observed). The day care adviser outlined the steps in the registration process and distributed the relevant application forms. The centre head described the services offered to childminders, notably its weekly drop-in sessions and toy library facilities. The experienced childminder explained her role as one of the 'link ladies' in the area – minders who acted as coordinators or representatives of others in their locality and who, by keeping informed of placements, could give information concerning vacancies to parents seeking day care.

The main training provision in Bracknell, however, was the pre-registration course, held at the Children's Centre, and planned and delivered by the social services day care advisers and the head of the centre. The course, consisting of six once-weekly evening sessions, was presented to would-be child minders as a requirement of the registration procedure. The workers, like colleagues in other areas who have adopted this strategy, acknowledged that they were on dubious legal ground in doing so, but added that refusal to attend was rare. The frequency of the courses had recently been increased to twice-termly, in order to deal with the large backlog of applicants for registration (100 at the start of the study).

Regulation of registration
The pre-registration course was seen by the local authority staff as, in part, a regulatory device. One adviser expressed it as 'a hurdle in the way of registration' which, it was hoped, might deter those who could not legally be refused registration, but about whose suitability the advisers felt some concern. In their view, committing oneself to coming out one evening a week for six weeks demonstrated a reassuring seriousness of approach to the task of childminding. No formal assessments were made of the participants, so that the regulatory strategy relied heavily on self-elimination. The assumption seemed to be that a realisation of all that childminding involved would deter not only those who were disillusioned by the discovery, but also those who might be, in some unspecified way, unsuitable.

According to one adviser, however, the course was not proving to be an effective sifting device, since few applicants failed to complete it. It is also unknown, of course, what action would be taken by those whose pursuit of registration was curtailed at this point, or to the many more who, as social services staff in other areas have reported, are persuaded to withdraw on the grounds of perceived unsuitability (Ferri and Birchall, 1987). Local authorities are unlikely to have the staff resources available to follow up such cases in order to establish whether those concerned do, indeed, abandon their intention to start or continue minding. The fact that a substantial proportion of applicants for registration are *already* caring for children (22 per cent of the 200 minders in our earlier study), suggests that such follow-up may be an important issue in the regulation of illegal childminding.

Awareness of the minder's role

A broad general aim of the pre-registration course in Bracknell was to familiarise applicants with the role of childminder, so that, as one worker put it 'they don't think it's just (*sic*) mothering in their house'. Thus, the course objectives placed emphasis on aspects of childminding which were not directly or merely child-related, and it was these other elements which were also seen by the advisers as linked to the course's further major aim – that of enhancing the status of childminding in the eyes of the participants:

'The whole theme is to raise the status of the minder – make them aware they're doing a worthwhile job – it isn't just (*sic*) looking after somebody's child.'

This recurrent use of the word 'just' in conjunction with 'mothering' and 'looking after children' can be seen as reflecting the low status which our society confers upon such work, and may partially explain why, in seeking to raise the image of childminding, the course also addressed other aspects of the minder's role. It is also important to note, however, that insofar as childminding was seen to resemble mothering, the trainers in Bracknell considered that the personal maternal experience of most applicants for registration removed the need and justification for addressing such areas of practice on the course.

The Bracknell course observed

As noted above, the venue for the pre-registration course in Bracknell was the NCH Children's Centre, which offered facilities in the form of a fairly spacious room in which comfortable chairs could be arranged in an informal circle. Fifteen applicants for registration attended the observed sessions, which began at 7.15 p.m. in a relaxed atmosphere with coffee and biscuits, and lasted for two hours. All but one, heavily pregnant, participant completed the course.

Each session was conducted by the head of the Children's Centre and a day care adviser, who also gave verbal presentations on the first three topics listed on the following course outline. This was distributed at the start to the participants. The last three sessions were delivered respectively by a speech therapist, health visitor and experienced childminder.

Outline of pre-registration course in Bracknell

Week 1   Introduction; aims of the course; video: 'Through the Eyes of a Child'

Week 2   Emotional care; the needs of child, parent and minder

Week 3   Play

Week 4   Speech and language development

Week 5   First aid and infectious diseases

Week 6   The business side of childminding

Except for the video shown on the first evening, the general format of the sessions consisted of a talk by one or more of the workers present, followed by a focused discussion, either among the whole group or several smaller groups which then reported back. In both settings, the level of contribution from participants, predictably, varied – with some much more vocal than others. Also, the discussion groups, while given specific issues to consider by the tutors, frequently developed into anecdotal exchanges of personal experiences, especially the characteristics and idiosyncracies of the participants' own children. This can, of course, provide a valuable and meaningful starting point for raising awareness of differences of view and behaviour which are of crucial importance in the context of childminding. To do so effectively, however, requires a considerable amount of time, skill and expertise – ingredients which are not easily harnessed in a brief course such as this.

Our observations of the courses in operation raised a number of important issues relating to the key topics of the quality of provision, relationships in childminding, and its business aspects. These will be examined in later chapters, which focus specifically on these matters, so that the points arising from the observations of training, and the findings emerging from our case studies, can be linked together to explore the impact of course provision on what actually took place in the childminding setting. We shall then go on to consider the implications of our empirical data for the future development of childminder training. At this stage, however, there are one or two general points to note about the pre-registration course in Bracknell.

The first concerns the problem presented by attempting to cover a series of wide-ranging and intricate topics within the constraints of six brief sessions. The course curriculum outlined above indicated breadth rather than depth of coverage, with the result that the intrinsic complexity of the subjects could not be adequately addressed. To take one example: the theoretical concept of children's play progressing through sequential levels from Solitary, Parallel, Onlooker, Joining-in (associative), Simple Cooperative through to Complex Cooperative, was briefly presented in juxtaposition with the assertion that development will take place 'in a natural way' given the 'right' situation, feelings and handling. Just what constituted this appropriate context was not examined, however, and it might be felt that the participants would emerge from the session rather more confused than enlightened.

It is also important to note that the mode of presentation of the pre-registration course in Bracknell highlighted the ambiguity of the social services department's position in relation to the private activity of childminding. Thus, while establishing attendance as a requirement for registration, itself a responsibility of the local authority, the tutors also explicitly disclaimed any role in setting or assessing standards of provision. This was particularly evident in respect of the actual ingredients of childcare; as noted above, the maternal experience of most applicants was seen as removing the need for – or practicability of – addressing such areas of practice. As one adviser put it when interviewed:

'we start off by telling them that we haven't asked them to come because we think they need to know about how to bring up children. They've probably all done it – and done it well!'

Indeed, in the course we observed, the tutors assured the participants that: 'we are not here to preach'. The group members were informed that it was *their* course and encouraged to feel free to comment and make suggestions as to what they would like it to cover. Assessment sheets for this purpose were completed at the end of each course, and, according to the workers, changes made in the light of these views. As one adviser put it: 'If something is a "no go area" we would cut it out'.

The underlying ambiguity in the social services department's position in relation to childminding, and those involved in it, was encapsulated in the comments to participants of one tutor on the course which we observed.

'Once the door's closed and you're on your own, only you know what's happening to those children. We've got to trust you and think that what you're doing is what the parents want.'

This would seem to imply that, in the private context of childminding arrangements, it is the *parents'* wishes which are to be followed. Yet, paradoxically it is the *local authority's* trust to which the childminder, in the above statement, is ultimately answerable; an agency which, as we have seen, accepts little responsibility for childminders as workers, or for establishing the standards of their provision. In designing and delivering training courses for childminders, day care advisers are placed firmly on the horns of this dilemma, and it might be felt that they themselves would benefit from some training opportunity to confront and deal with the contradictions in their own position.

Waltham Forest

The other location for the study was one of the three divisions of the London Borough of Waltham Forest. Situated in the north-east of the metropolitan area, the borough contained wide socio-economic variations. The northern part was suburban and comparatively affluent in character, while the southern division, which was chosen for the study, was more typical of an inner London borough, with streets of Victorian terraced housing and a number of council estates, including some tower blocks and deck access dwellings. It was also an ethnically diverse area, with a sizeable population of Asian or Afro-Caribbean origin.

Policy and practice

The workers with day-to-day responsibility for childminding were the Childminding Coordinators (something of a misnomer since their duties also included day nurseries), with one full-time and one part-time post based in each of the two area social work offices. Although this arrangement was considered advantageous in terms of local accessibility for the public, its acknowledged shortcomings included a lack of specialist knowledge of child development among the senior social workers with line management responsibility for the coordinators. Another was the inevitably low priority accorded to childminding as, in the words of one senior manager, 'a universal service' among the more pressing demands made upon a social work team. These included, in particular, the needs of a rising elderly population and a sharp increase in cases of child abuse. There was a growing, unmet demand for childminding; one area, for example, had only 90 registered childminders and a currently estimated need for up to 40 more. Paradoxically, there was also a huge backlog of applicants awaiting registration (140 at the start of the study) – an extremely slow (up to 18 months) process due to limited staff resources and, in particular, a recent cut-back in clerical support.

Of the four coordinators in post when the study began, two had social science degrees (one, additionally, held a CQSW), one was a qualified teacher and the fourth had NNEB training. Their previous work experience included nursery teaching, day nurseries, play-groups and educational home visiting. In addition, one coordinator had followed the London Boroughs' Training Scheme on teaching short courses to childminders, and another had received in-service training in counselling and assessment.

Another key worker in the childminding service was a senior social worker (Under-Fives – Childminding), a borough-wide post whose occupant held a degree in Psychology, a Master's Degree in Child Development, and had previously worked for a national voluntary agency and another London borough. She had played an influential role in developing policy, practice and training in relation to childminding in Waltham Forest, and in providing professional advice and support to the coordinators.

Despite the relatively low priority which it was seen to occupy within the framework of social work teams, childminding – and, indeed, *all* day care services – were considerably better resourced in Waltham Forest than in Bracknell. In addition to two day nurseries in the division studied, the borough had for some years operated a childminding subsidy scheme, which offered direct financial support to families in social need and/or on low incomes. As we shall see, the greater involvement of the local authority in direct service provision in Waltham Forest was matched by more explicit departmental objectives in the approach to childminder training.

Training: aims and approaches
Although Waltham Forest had a long history of involvement in childminder training, a comparatively recent development was a pre-registration course. A major impetus for its introduction was, in the words of one of the coordinators, to 'get hold of the registration

situation' by processing the long list of applicants more speedily and effectively. It was felt that a number of important issues were more easily addressed in a group context, which also enabled the social services workers to reduce the number and length of home visits made in connection with registration.

The main aim of the course in terms of content, however, was described by all the coordinators involved as 'mutual assessment'. Its specific objectives were clearly set out in a detailed evaluative report on the pilot courses prepared by the senior social worker (Under-Fives – Childminding) who, with the coordinators, had planned and delivered them. These are summarised as follows:

'*to assess childminding applicants*
... an opportunity to see the applicants in a group setting and to see how they respond to a variety of material.

to share expectations about the role of a childminder in a multiracial and multicultural borough
... aims to give a clear message ... that Waltham Forest is an "equal opportunities" borough, whose services are available to all families ... Course leaders are looking for a willingness on the part of applicants to examine the issues, for many of them this will be for the first time, and to work with us.

for the applicant, finding out about the job: Is it for me?
... aims to give applicants a clear picture of what the department's expectations of childminders are, what meeting parents' wishes involves and whether they are prepared to do this, how childminding affects their family, their own need for support to do the job and the business side of childminding and how to protect themselves as workers, eg contracts, insurance etc.

establishing a working relationship: potential childminders/childminding co-ordinators/Social Services Department
...it is important to give applicants a realistic picture of the department's work and to ensure that they are familiar with some faces at the Area team.

raising awareness of professional issues
... applicants need to be aware of what the department considers to be good under fives child care practice, to have an opportunity to examine how caring for someone else's child is different from caring for one's own child, to examine current ideas on caring for young children and to update themselves if necessary, to consider what providing anti-sexist, anti-racist care means in practice, to examine the issues around working with families under stress, confidentiality etc.'

Many of the aims summarised above echo those articulated by the advisory workers in Bracknell. However, there were also a number of important differences, which seemed to reflect a more interventionist stance on the part of the London borough in respect of the service for which it was responsible.

The most obvious example, perhaps, was Waltham Forest's anti-racist policy. This was referred to by all the staff interviewed for the study. In the words of one area manager:

'the most urgent task is to make services more responsive to local – especially Black – communities. We're not meeting the needs of Black people. We don't have enough information about what these groups need – yet most children in day nurseries are Black and the staff are White. We fail to offer the right role models, environment, activities. A Black perspective is not incorporated into the work we do.'

While pointing to the need to recruit more childminders from the minority ethnic communities, several workers also commented that Afro-Caribbean parents, in particular, preferred day nursery to childminder provision. The perceived reasons included the lower cost (there was a flat rate charge for places in the authority's nurseries), the more 'educational' orientation of group care and, as one coordinator put it, the 'horrendous childminding situations' which many Black parents may have themselves experienced as children in the 1960s and early 1970s.

The senior social worker (Under-Fives – Childminding) had sought to incorporate the borough's anti-racist policy into its under-fives work, and, more specifically, into the childminding pre-registration course.

'There was nothing happening on under fives. I thought that, as a department, we should be making a clear statement – not just asking minders if they are willing to accept Black children, but looking beyond that to what providing childminding in a borough like Waltham Forest actually *means*.'

As a result of these initiatives, joint guidelines had been produced with the local Childminding Association which had become what one Principal Officer described as the 'cornerstone of registration policy'.

'If someone refused to take children from certain groups, or expressed views that we feel are unsuitable to place a child with, we won't register.'

Actually implementing such a policy, however, was less easy, as exemplified in the coordinators' account of the task of assessing applicants for registration. At the end of every session of the pre-registration course, tutors completed an assessment on each participant in respect of the topics covered. The criteria employed were, according to one worker, whether applicants:

'had a good idea of what meeting children's needs involved, and were prepared to do it; were sympathetic to parents' wishes; and were open to working with us – open to ideas'.

As one of her colleagues pointed out, actually making such assessments could be problematic – especially in relation to issues such as anti-racism where:

'we are asking people to review their fundamental attitudes. It's hard to assess whether we've made any headway. Our whole cultural ethos is about giving the answers that people want to hear. If you give off any clue about what you want people to say – particularly about anti-racism – they'll come out with the answers they feel you want and it may not reflect their true views or what they actually do in their own homes. Those are the issues its hardest for us to put over effectively, make any change, and indicate whether we *have* made any change.'

The Waltham Forest course observed

Unlike Bracknell, the pre-registration course in Waltham Forest took place in the mornings. It was also slightly shorter, consisting of five weekly sessions of two hours' duration. Various venues had been tried, but the coordinators favoured a local day nursery, which, they felt, 'helped minders feel supported and valued by the department'. Actually arranging this could frequently be problematic however – indeed, the course that we observed had to be postponed for several weeks until suitable premises were available. It finally took place in the small, but comfortable, staff room of one of the borough's day nurseries, where crèche facilities were also provided.

Nine applicants for registration attended the first session of the course and seven of them completed it. Five of these were of White British origin and two were Afro-Caribbean. The course was tutored by the senior social worker (Under-Fives – Childminding) and the two day care coordinators in the area concerned. The general style was similar to that in Bracknell, with topics raised in short presentations by the tutors and pursued in discussion by the participants, either as a group or in twos or threes. The general impression gained from observation was that the smaller number of participants on the Waltham Forest course created a more intimate atmosphere and facilitated contribution to whole-group discussion, especially among its shyer, more reticent members. Another distinguishing feature of the Waltham Forest course was the setting of a homework task at the end of each session. Participants were asked to read, consider or work through specific topics or questions, and a brief review and feedback formed the introduction to further consideration of the issue in the subsequent session. A written summary of the aims and content of the course was distributed to the participants at the first session. The aims listed corresponded to the five headings referred to in the summary on page 46, while topics to be covered at each session were as follows:

Session 1   Introductions. Expectations of childminders. Why choose childminding? Safety. Homework: safety checklist and First Aid questionnaire.

Session 2   Film: 'Infants at work'. Children: ages and stages. Play. Homework: water play; questionnaire: looking after other people's children.

Session 3   Film: 'The eye of the storm'. The effects of racism on children and families. Childminding in a multiracial, multicultural borough. Homework: questionnaire: What's naughty and why? questionnaire: Who is what?

Session 4   Boys and girls. What's naughty and why? Discipline, setting limits. Non-accidental injury. Parents. Homework: What about the parents? Planning a childminding week.

Session 5   What about the parents? Meeting parents' wishes. The working day. The business side of childminding. Assessment of the course.

As in the account of the Bracknell course, issues emerging from our observations of training in relation to key aspects of the childminding situation will be examined in the chapters dealing with the topics concerned. Here, as before, one or two similar, general points regarding the Waltham Forest course need to be noted.

First, like their Bracknell colleagues, the Waltham Forest trainers were faced with the problem of seeking to cover an extensive curriculum in a very short time. As the foregoing list shows, the course content included a number of difficult and sensitive subjects such as race and gender. However, the limited time allocated to them permitted only cursory coverage, and, on a number of occasions, comments by participants which indicated views or practices which might be problematic in a childminding situation were not probed or examined in any great depth. It was the coordinators' stated practice to pursue such matters with the person concerned during a subsequent home visit. However, while this might prove effective in relation to an individual applicant, other course members could be left uncertain as to the authority's position on key issues.

The higher profile adopted by the London borough (by comparison with the county authority) in the development of a childcare policy was nonetheless reflected in both the content and the presentation of the course. As well as explaining the borough's policy, in particular its anti-racist stance, the coordinators introduced themselves as coming from the area social services offices, from which childminders would be *supervised*, and explicity referred to the assessment function of the course, as part of the registration process. Yet this would seem to indicate a certain amount of conflict in the role of the coordinators as trainers. As assessors of would-be childminders they are clearly in a powerful position *vis-à-vis* the course members. At the same time, the ethos of adult education, within which such courses operate, demands a minimum of distance between facilitators and participants. Coordinators were thus trying to create a relationship of equality with participants which their role as assessors effectively precluded. Furthermore, the assessment function of the course was somewhat at odds with another explicit stated objective: namely, to aid applicants in deciding whether they really wanted to become childminders. The knowledge that they were being assessed might well inhibit participants from raising issues of concern or expressing their true views – an outcome which would be counterproductive to the achievement of both training aims.

The college course in Waltham Forest

Our study of childminder training in Waltham Forest focused particularly on the aims and approaches of the pre-registration course, including observing it in operation. However, it is also important to mention a more long-established training strategy in the borough, namely, a course for more experienced practitioners based at the local Further Education college. This had been held at intervals for over 10 years, consisted of 10-12 weekly three-hour sessions, and was tutored by college staff and the coordinators. Invitations to participate were extended by the social services workers to those who expressed particular interest, to other practising childminders who had not attended the pre-registration course, and to a third group whose practice gave the coordinators some cause for concern. Some topics on the curriculum, such as First Aid and children with special needs, were included in response to minders' requests, but the course was also seen by the social services workers as an opportunity to update childminders on significant developments in the department's policy – for example, procedures for dealing with child abuse.

Official involvement with parents

Before concluding our account of childminding policy and practice within the two local authorities in the study, it is important to look briefly at the role each played in relation to parents seeking day care. Although, as noted earlier, social services departments have no formal responsibility for what is seen as a private arrangement between childminder and parent, there is, in practice, wide variation between different areas in the nature of the agency's involvement with the consumers of this type of day care.

Bracknell

According to a senior manager in Bracknell, a future goal, contained in the division's three-year plan, was to develop the under fives section as a 'resource centre where the public or agencies can come for information and advice on available services'. In current practice, however, contact between day care advisers and parents was normally limited to telephone conversations when parents seeking day care approached the department. Details would then be obtained of their child's age, address, the hours wanted, and any preferences regarding smoking and pets. In general, the advisers would then give the names and phone numbers of any apparently suitable minder known to have a vacancy and/or refer the parent to the local 'link lady', who, as mentioned previously, was an experienced child-minder acting as coordinator for others in her own area. According to the advisers, they would urge parents to visit several possible minders before making a selection but, as a matter of policy, would avoid *recommending* anyone, on the grounds that the choice was a personal matter. As one adviser explained: 'I don't know what they're looking for'.

Nonetheless, there was some evidence from their comments that, consciously or sub-consciously, the advisers' values and judgements sometimes played a part in determining who was put in touch with whom.

'I must admit, sometimes you can tell when talking to someone... what type of background they've had... education-wise... there might be some people you'd perhaps avoid giving their names... people from totally different backgrounds.'

Comments such as these point to a rather more interventionist approach on the part of social services workers than their declared policy would suggest.

Waltham Forest

A further point of difference between Waltham Forest and Bracknell in the operation of the childminding service lay in the London borough workers' greater involvement with parents seeking day care. All parents requesting provision would be invited to an initial interview with a childminding coordinator. Except for families with two working parents who were requesting a childminder, rather than day nursery provision, and who would not qualify for a subsidy, all applications would then be forwarded to a day care panel.

At the initial interview with parents, the coordinators would record details of the child's age, future school catchment area and particular requests or preferences concerning matters such as diet, smoking and the presence of pets, for, as one worker put it, 'ours is a matching service'. While such factors are likely to be of great importance to some parents, it is also worth noting that, in contrast to questions of childcare practice, attitudes and values, they are matters on which it is relatively easy for childminding workers to obtain information. Attempts to match parents and childminders also extended to ethnic and cultural characteristics so that, for example, 'if an Asian family whose first language was Urdu, or a Black West Indian family strongly wanted the same, we'd do our best to offer that'.

In addition to the above factors, however, the workers also pointed out that 'you try to choose somebody with similar ideas of child care – that's the crucial thing', although they acknowledged that it was very difficult in one interview to make valid judgements about what people really wanted.

In practice, however, it appeared that the 'matching service' was not always as effective as the social services workers would have wished. The most obvious reason was the inadequate supply of childminders, which meant that there was frequently little or no choice available.

'It depends on vacancies – sometimes it's nonsense to say we match people – if there are 50 waiting and (a minder's) near enough – they'll go.'

Another influential factor was, in the view of the coordinators, the parents' own feelings of discomfort about approaching and selecting a potential childminder.

'It depends how confident they are – lots of parents will take the first one, because the whole thing of going round asking questions is so traumatic.'

Despite the constraints upon operating an effective matching service, it was clear that parents seeking day care in Waltham Forest received considerably more information and advice than did their counterparts in Bracknell. At the initial interview, the coordinators would go through the childminding contract with them, and also stress the need to discuss a wide range of issues with potential childminders, both giving and asking for information which was important to them in finding satisfactory day care.

There was not, however, complete consensus among the workers interviewed in Waltham Forest about what the role of the local authority *should* be in relation to parents. One Principal Officer criticised the *principle* of trying to match parents and childminders, considering that this represented a fostering model which was inappropriate to 'mainstream' childminding. In her view, parents who approached the social services department with a straightforward request for a minder 'should be given a list and go out and select. I wouldn't want someone telling *me*'. Childminding, she felt, had been:

'slow in catching on that we're in the age of consumerism – parents go round different schools, so why do we have to be selecting a minder for them?'

Another concern voiced by a senior social worker was that the coordinators' involvement with the parental side of day care made serious inroads upon limited staff resources.

'They should be predominantly supporting the service – recruiting minders – but often get encroached upon by the needs of parents.'

The somewhat conflicting perspectives revealed here are further symptoms of the ambiguity surrounding the role of the local authority in relation to childminding; in particular the public/private dualism concerning the service. As the Waltham Forest workers' views indicate, it is by no means clear where the boundaries of the social services departments' responsibilities lie in relation to child-minders, parents and children as the chief protagonists in day care arrangements.

'Sometimes we've got very confused in childminding about who our client is.'

The perceived importance of training for childcare

Before concluding this chapter, it is useful to consider the general response of childminders in the study – and the parents who used their services – to the whole notion of training for this type of day care.

The childminders' view of training

All of the care providers who had been on courses of some kind claimed to have found them interesting and useful. The aspect which they had most valued, however, was the insight offered into what childminding actually involved and its possible pitfalls. Thus, a Bracknell minder expressed appreciation that the pre-registration course 'lets you know more of what you are in for' – a view echoed by a colleague in Waltham Forest who observed that: 'it does help you make up your mind whether you want to be a childminder or not'.

A rather different picture emerged when respondents were asked if they considered that training was a *necessary* preparation for childminding. In almost every case, the question was construed in terms of childcare skills, and the majority (two-thirds) expressed the firm view that, in the light of their experience as mothers, such a measure was not required.

'Not if you're a mother – if you've got children it's pure commonsense really. You have brought up kids of your own and as such you don't need training.'

Such statements contain an implicit perception about the nature of childminding as domestic, family-based care, and the role of the childminder as comparable to mothering. This was expressed in more explicit terms by a number of interviewees.

'I think the best training of all is that you should have had children of your own, because I think childminding is just another branch of being a mum!'

'I think being a mother is quite enough. I don't classify myself as a teacher – when the children come here they're not in a school, they're not in a nursery – they're in a *home*.'

To the extent that childminders see their maternal experience as sufficient preparation for their work, there are at least two major reasons why they are likely to resist the notion of training for childcare. The first involves the perception of mothering, or parenting, as instinctive behaviour for which training is irrelevant.

'If you are a parent anyway, it is all built in – a natural instinct – something that is *there*. When you have actually had a child you know what to do with children I think.'

Secondly, at a more personal level, it would appear that childminders are unlikely to be readily receptive to training messages which challenge or conflict with their own values and behaviour as parents.

This was nowhere more evident that in relation to the topic of physical punishment of children, a practice which was unequivocally proscribed on the pre-registration courses in each area and, in Waltham Forest, reinforced by a local authority letter to all registered minders. In each locality, several respondents made it clear during the interview that they disagreed with and disregarded a policy which was at odds with their own parenting practice. As one Waltham Forest minder put it 'I bring them up just like I bring my own up – if they're naughty, I smack them'. A colleague in Bracknell described how, on the pre-registration course:

'when I mentioned that I give the child a smack (adviser) had a shock. She said, "You must not touch a child – it's wrong". But I don't believe that – and I had all the childminders behind me – they all do the same sort of thing.'

It should be noted here, however, that such views are by no means characteristic of all childminders. Indeed, vigorous lobbying by grassroots organisations was influential in having childminders included in the section of the Children Act 1989 which stated that physical punishment of children in care facilities 'should not be used'.

Given the somewhat ambiguous position which childminder training occupies in the broader policy context, it was hardly surprising to find that its recipients expressed a diversity of views regarding the significance of such training. At one extreme were those who felt that having attended a course conferred upon them some official stamp of approval. One respondent who had followed the pre-registration course in Waltham Forest felt that 'at the end you're qualified', and a counterpart in Bracknell stated that she had received (a certificate) 'to say I'd passed in childminding skills'.

At the other end of the spectrum were course participants who were somewhat more sceptical of the value of the experience. A Waltham Forest minder observed that 'they haven't got enough facilities to train you really', while a Bracknell colleague expressed criticism that the pre-registration course there:

'didn't examine any of us. It was based on all 16 of us. I think they should spend some time with us as individuals, because they need to get to know what we're like as a person to do the childminding. I got a certificate but no one there really knows me.'

Such comments as these indicate how important it is to assess the significance of training within the context of the local authority structure in which childminding is located. The lack of power and resources which would enable social services departments to provide effective support and supervision for childminders inevitably weakens the status and potential impact of training initiatives.

The parental view of training

No investigation to date has sought the opinions of those who use childminders' services as to the importance of training for such work. It was interesting to discover, therefore, that the views of the parents in our sample revealed a very different perception to those expressed by the providers. Whereas two-thirds of the childminders considered that training was not necessary, it was revealing to discover that a similar proportion of parents were convinced that it was. In the same vein, while childminders tended to think that childcare was the one topic on which they did not require training, this was, in their clients' view, the major reason why it was important. For many parents, the thought that the person caring for their child had attended a course on the subject was a welcome source of reassurance that the care would be competent.

'It's important, especially when it comes to hygiene... it's good to have a childminder who knows how to deal with your children, how to talk to them and play with them.'

'A very good idea – especially if it can sort of gear them to the idea of how to encourage play, imagination – you know, stuff like that.'

Few parents, however, had any detailed knowledge of the courses available to childminders in their area, and, as with the providers, there was little consensus among them as to what the experience of training actually signified. Some, like the following Bracknell couple, considered that the motivation to attend a course was, in itself, a positive indication.

Father: 'I think that shows the person has a sense of commitment.'
Mother: 'That she views it as a job to be taken seriously.'
Father: 'I think it gives you a sense of security in that person.'

Similarly, a mother in Waltham Forest expressed the view that 'if you go through the training you are definitely going to be dedicated'. Other parents, however, were less convinced that training was any guarantee of competence or quality.

'She might go through all the course, but she really doesn't know how... so you have to be really trusting.'

'She's told me about the films she's seen on children – whether she'd ever put that into practice or not I don't know... Sometimes you can see a thing and think that's a good idea, but you never actually do it.'

Our study's findings have thus indicated very different views on the part of the users and providers of childminding as to whether training for the childcare component of the work is appropriate or necessary. There were also marked differences of opinion *within* each group regarding what experience of the training currently available actually demonstrated about its recipients. This confused picture is, perhaps, understandable in the light of the ambivalent policy context in which childminder training is at present delivered. This is a key point in the analysis of its impact, and one to which we shall return in the final chapter.

Conclusions

The foregoing account of the approaches of the two local authorities in the study to childminding in general, and training in particular, has illustrated the ambiguities and tensions inherent in the official framework which surrounds this form of day care. In Bracknell, especially, policy and practice had been powerfully influenced by the view of childminding as a private activity, a view which undermines the validity of seeking to address issues of child care practice in the context of training. Thus, as one of the Bracknell advisers put it:

'It's a case of not imposing your standards of care into another person's situation – we don't know the mums and their standards – what their homes are like.'

In Waltham Forest, the authority's stronger, more interventionist position was exemplified by its overall policy on childcare, rooted in the notion of equality of race and gender, and extending to all the borough's services for children. This policy provided the basis for a more explicit training strategy with regard to childcare in the childminding situation.

In each area, the training courses which we observed sought to cover a wide range of complex and, in many cases, sensitive topics in a very short space of time. This put a great deal of pressure on the workers responsible and was an obstacle to an in-depth exploration of views, values and behaviour which could be of considerable significance for the provision of satisfactory day care. Nonetheless, the courses did raise a variety of salient issues and conveyed a number of important messages for practice in respect of the different aspects of childminding arrangements. Just what these were, and how they related to what took place in the conduct of our 30 sample cases, will be the focus of attention in the following chapters.

5. The start of the arrangements

In this chapter we look at how the parents and childminders in our sample found each other and set up the day care arrangements that were the subject of the study. What were parents seeking; what did childminders offer; and how well did these two components blend together as the basis for mutual satisfaction? We were also interested, however, in the *public* dimension to what has already been described as essentially a matter for *private* negotiation. The following account thus explores the part played by social services workers in bringing providers and users of day care into contact with one another and, of particular importance to this study, the contribution of childminder training to the potentially crucial stage of setting the framework for a new day care arrangement.

We begin, however, with a brief picture of the 60 families involved in the study. It should be remembered that this was not, nor was it intended to be, in any sense a representative sample of childminders or parents. Rather, it was deliberately chosen to include a *range* of characteristics and circumstances among both providers and users of day care so that the operation of childminding, and the impact of childminder training, could be examined in a number of different contexts.

The families: users and providers

The 'user' half of our sample consisted of 30 families containing 34 'target' children (20 girls and 14 boys), who had recently been placed with a childminder. The age distribution of the children, shown in Table 5.1, was heavily weighted towards the younger end of the pre-school age range; a factor no doubt partially explained by our sampling strategy of selecting new childminding arrangements.

Table 5.1 Age distribution of minded children

Age	Number
under 6 months	9
6 months – 1 year	6
1 – 2 years	7
2 – 3 years	5
3 – 4 years	6
school age	1
Total	34

In three of the families, a pair of siblings had simultaneously entered a new day care arrangement, and in a fourth, a six-month-old baby was placed with a minder who had already been looking after his three-year-old sister for some time. Apart from these three families, only six others contained more than one child, so that 21 of the 34 'targets' were first-born, only children. This contrasted with only five one-child families among the childminders, a factor which, as we shall see, was of some importance to both users and providers in their respective approaches to the day care situation. The minders' children were also somewhat older; the great majority were of school age, although seven of the 30 minders had pre-school children of their own.

The number and ages of children in the sample families were, predictably, related to the ages of the adults; so that the childminders tended to be older than the mothers of the children placed in their care. In cases where the age gap was wide, this, too, will be seen to be influential in the developing relationships between minder, parent and child. Although our sample was small, it is interesting to note that, in terms of age, the Bracknell childminders resembled those drawn from a comparable area in Oxfordshire study, with 12 of the 15 in their mid-30's (Bryant and others, 1980); while their peers in Waltham Forest had a wider age range (23 to 52), similar to the sample in the inner London boroughs studied by Mayall and Petrie (1983). This no doubt reflects the greater homogeneity in the population of the new town, with its concentration of young families.

There was no similar contrast between the two areas, however, in the length of time in which the groups of childminders had been providing day care. Almost half (13 of the 30) had been minding for less than two years, and nearly a third (nine) for five years or more.

Our sample thus contained a rather higher proportion of relatively inexperienced childminders than had our own earlier investigation (Ferri and Birchall, 1987) or the Oxfordshire and London studies (Bryant and others, op. cit.; Mayall and Petrie op. cit.). This was doubtless due to the fact that experience of training was an important criterion for inclusion in the sample, and was more likely to apply to recent entrants to the field.

As indicated in Chapter 2, 22 of the 30 childminders, 11 in each area, had attended a childminding course of some kind. Table 5.2 shows the numbers who had followed the particular courses described in the previous chapter.

Table 5.2 Number of childminders attending specific courses in each area

Type of course	Bracknell	Waltham Forest
pre-registration – observed by researchers	2	2
pre-registration – other	8	3
college-based course	1*	6
	11	11

*This was a child development course at a local Further Education college which was available to Bracknell childminders prior to the introduction of the current training programme focusing specifically on childminding.

Among the user families in the sample, there were five households comprising mother and child(ren) only (two in Bracknell, three in Waltham Forest). Four of the childminders (all in the London borough) were also mothers living alone with their children. In no case, however, did the childminding arrangement involve a single mother on both sides.

Racial background

There was a considerable contrast between the two study areas in terms of racial background. As already indicated in Chapter 4, Waltham Forest contained a rich diversity of racial and cultural groups and our sample was deliberately chosen in order that this should be represented, as the figures in Table 5.3 indicate.

Table 5.3 Racial background of families in Waltham Forest sample

Racial background	Parent sample	Minder sample
White British	6	8
Black British	2	0
Afro-Caribbean	2	2
European/White British	2	0
Black British/White British	1	0
Other British	1	1
Ghanaian	1	0
West Indian	0	1
Indian	0	1
Sri Lankan	0	1
Fijian	0	1
	15	15

In Bracknell, by contrast, almost all of the parents described themselves as White British, except for one couple who were both of European origin, two mothers who referred to having a Jewish background, and another who described her own background as English and whose child was of mixed parentage. Similarly, the minder sample in Bracknell included just one of European origin and one who had been born in the West Indies.

When it came to obtaining information on this subject, we felt it was essential to focus on the respondent's own perceptions. Thus, they were first asked an open-ended question regarding their racial background or origins. It is interesting and important to record that a number of White interviewees appeared unclear and uneasy about what was meant by the term 'racial'. Subsequently in the interview, all respondents were shown a card containing ethnic categories based on those adopted for the population census. In the figures presented above, wherever there was a discrepancy between answers to the two items, priority has been given to the reply to the open-ended question.

Table 5.4 shows the rich mix of racial backgrounds which had been brought together by the new childminding arrangements that we were studying.

Table 5.4 Racial background of families in sample cases

Parents' racial background	Minders' racial background	
	White British	*Other*
White British	17 cases	4 cases
		minders' background:
		Sri Lankan (1)
		Indian (1)
		European (1)
		West Indian (1)
Other	5 cases	4 cases
	parents' background:	*parents' background* *minders' background*
	Ghanaian (1)	Afro-Carib Fijian
	Black British (1)	Jewish West Indian
	Afro-Caribbean (1)	Black British Afro-Caribbean
	Other European (1)	Black British/
	Other (1)	White British Afro-Caribbean

The respondents were not asked directly whether racial background was an important factor in the day care placement. One Afro-Caribbean mother, however, explained that she wanted her young son 'to learn to identify in a very positive way with Black people, whether it be Black or Asian'. In her choice of a Fijian childminder, she felt that the caregiver's lifestyle and approach to children would be more akin to her own than that in a traditional White British home.

One Black couple, who had placed their child with a White minder, had told the childminding coordinator that the minder's racial background was unimportant. So, too, had a White mother and father with a Sri Lankan childminder; their only concern had been that the childminder's household should be English-speaking, so that their child, exposed to both English and French at home, should not become linguistically confused.

Interestingly, another White British mother who had chosen an Indian childminder emphasised that she 'wouldn't want someone who wasn't *aware* of racism and sexism because that is quite important to me' and another, Jewish, mother with a West Indian minder explained that she 'would not want a minder who was racist... because we're not quite White'. In such cases, it appeared that the childminder's own racial background had given parents reassurance concerning the values that were important to them.

Social class background

Looking at social class background in terms of the occupations of the adults in the sample revealed that, in both study areas, almost half of the mothers using childminding were employed in professional fields. These included no fewer than seven teachers, a doctor, a lawyer, a psychologist and a social worker. Other mothers held a variety of administrative and secretarial posts. The fathers' occupations showed a similar pattern with, again, almost half engaged in professional or managerial positions. The picture concerning the providers of day care was rather different, however, with only a quarter of the childminders' husbands or partners having professional or managerial occupations. The day care arrangements being studied thus brought together, in a number of cases, two families from different socio-economic groups, further reflected in some instances, in the location and nature of their respective accommodation. No direct questions on this topic were put to respondents, and in only three cases, did the views expressed indicate that social class background had been a salient factor in the arrangement of day care. These involved parents who were anxious to place their children in homes which they felt were similar in this respect to their own.

The overall picture presented by the foregoing description of the families was thus one of considerable diversity both *within* the groups of users and providers of day care, and also *between* them in terms of the characteristics of family composition, social and racial background which were brought together by the formation of the childminding arrangements.

Why day care was needed

In every case but one, day care was required to provide for children whose parents – or, more accurately, mothers – were in, or about to commence, paid employment. (This single case involved a mother who was only prompted to look for a job when an acquaintance, in the process of registering as a childminder, offered to look after her daughter.) In no fewer than 13 of the 30 cases, the new day care placement had been sought in anticipation of the mother's planned return to work after taking maternity leave, and all but one of these concerned a first-born child. A further seven arrangements involved older pre-school children whose mothers were re-entering the labour market after a longer period at home. In the remaining third of the sample, the children had already experienced day care, and these new placements followed the termination of a previous minding arrangement. Almost all of these had ended at the childminders' instigation: four had become pregnant, two gave up due to health problems and another two for domestic reasons.

Altogether 13 of the 30 families had had previous childminding placements, and seven of these had experienced more than one. Four had had two previous arrangements, and three children were being placed with their fourth childminder. Again, according to the parents, almost all of these arrangements had been terminated by the childminder. Without interviewing the childminders concerned we cannot, of course, be certain about the circumstances in which the placements ended. However, if the parents' accounts are accurate, this would seem to suggest an element of instability and unreliability in the supply side of this private day care market.

There were thus highly contrasting contexts in which the arrangements we studied had been sought, and these, as we shall see, played an important part in determining how they started and developed. There was also great variation, however, in the circumstances which had led to the mothers' decision to seek paid work and the parents' feelings about their situation. For almost everyone interviewed, financial considerations had played at least a part in the mother's return to employment. In half a dozen cases it was the sole reason; the parents concerned would have preferred the mother to be at home with their children, but two incomes were seen as necessary to attain their aspirations, or at least an acceptable standard of living.

'We wouldn't be able to live here if I wasn't working.... we wanted to get on and do things and it needed both of our wages.'

'If we had enough money I would stay at home with him and have another one tomorrow!'

The stress and conflict experienced by many parents as they strive to reconcile the demands of work and family life is clearly evident in the following excerpt from an initial interview.

Mother: 'I didn't really want to go back I must admit...if we could afford to, I wouldn't work.'

Father: 'It's just very... demanding.'

Mother: 'Yes – I find it very difficult to fit everything in. And I worry that when I'm older I'll think, "Oh, I wish I'd been at home with them when they were tiny".'

Father: 'Well, it also creates a problem for *me*. Because I can choose my hours, but the less hours I do the less soon I'm going to be earning the money that will enable (mother) to be at home. And I suppose there's a certain amount of guilt there – in that I can't organise it so it takes the workload off (mother).'

In other families, however, the economic pressure to work was accompanied by a positive wish on the mother's part to enter or continue in employment. As the following comments from three different mothers indicate, this could involve a complex combination of views and motives, including a desire for financial independence, to make progress in a career, or a disinclination towards a home-bound existence.

'It's nice to feel I have an income that is *mine*. Mine to contribute to the family – not to spend on myself but to contribute. I value that.'

'I'd reached a stage in my career where I'd just been promoted and I knew that if I gave up as soon as (child) was born... and spent three to five years at home with her, when I re-entered teaching, I would have to start all over again.'

'Personally I can't stand to stay indoors day in day out looking after a child. I want to go out and do something with myself – I was here for a year or so and I was just going crazy.'

Mothers who were positively motivated to work outside the home for one or more of the above reasons also expressed the view that it was in their children's interests that they should not be confined together on a full-time basis. This is not to say, however, that they had found the decision straightforward or free of conflict. Several mothers who had taken maternity leave and were convinced that returning to work was the right course to take, nonetheless felt torn when actually it came to doing so.

'I was in two minds in the run-up... I would be missing out on all the fun times. By the time the second six months came round I wasn't itching to go back, I was actually enjoying being (at home).'

The fathers concerned, while sharing and supporting their partners' decisions regarding work, tended to see the ensuing emotional conflict as something which mothers themselves had to resolve. As one mother related:

'Although I asked (husband) what he thought, he said, "Well, it's really your decision, because it's you that's got to go through it and do it".'

Despite the increasing social approval accorded to maternal employment, it was evident from the accounts given by many mothers in our study that they received little support in dealing with the contradictory pressures which they experienced. In some cases, their own parents had expressed dismay at their rejection of full-time motherhood. One mother related how her family:

'felt very strongly about (child) going out of the family to someone else... I could have done with the support from that end and I wasn't getting it.'

Another was criticised by a friend who said:

'"Oh – you're a bad mother sending your child off to this childminder – you ought to be at home with her." And I thought, "Oh God – everything she's said is true!"'

One mother appeared to receive somewhat contradictory messages from her own partner, who, during the interview, expressed the wish that she could stay at home and 'be a great mother/daughter combination' but also that he didn't want her to 'give up her profession and be a doting mum like a friend of ours'. It is none too surprising, therefore, that the mother in question summed up the feelings of many of those in the study when she said:

'You can't help feeling guilty whatever you do... you end up convincing yourself that she's having an opportunity.'

The extreme dilemma which mothers may experience in this situation was illustrated by another interviewee who recalled how she felt 'terrible' when she left her baby son with a childminder, and then felt guilty again when she realised she hadn't been thinking about him while she was occupied at work!

Childminders' views on working mothers

In the light of the powerful, often ambivalent feelings experienced by mothers in relation to their return to employment and the use of day care, it was important to explore the views on this subject of the childminders who would be providing that care. In our earlier interview study involving 200 childminders we found that, when asked for their opinions on maternal employment, 80 per cent expressed approval, or at least uncritical acceptance. Similarly, when the childminders in the present study were questioned on the same topic, their replies tended to be non-judgemental in respect of mothers who chose, or were obliged, to go out to work and seek day care. But the perceptions underlying this apparent tolerance are rather more complex, as illustrated by the following excerpts from an interview with a childminder:

'Everybody's different aren't they? I've got... no sort of bad feelings about women leaving their children... it's up to every individual. I know it can't be easy – to leave a tiny baby – it must be heartbreaking! (But)... it didn't ever occur to me to leave my daughter with anyone – I just wanted to do it myself.'

The concepts contained in the above remarks – of the *abandonment* of a child, of the *pain* of the implied rupturing of the mother-child bond and non-fulfilment of the mothering role – are both powerful and pervasive in the accounts of the childminders in our study. The immediate responses which many childminders give when asked why they embarked upon the activity – for example, the need or desire to earn some money, a liking for involvement with children – often conceal an unspoken assumption that they *had* to be at home to care for their own children. When asked for their views on mothers working, most of the minders in our study began by voicing at least neutral opinions, then immediately added that they could not have contemplated such action themselves.

'I don't think I could have done it. I could not have left my son with someone I didn't know.'

'I didn't want to – I don't think I *could* do it – I wouldn't think they were *mine* – they would pick up everybody else's... habits and that... there isn't anybody else I'd *like* enough for my boys to stay with... maybe I shouldn't say that!' (laughed)

'I don't know how they *can* go straight back to work.... I would have felt guilty going out to work if I wasn't there for them when they came home.'

Such views were expressed by all but a handful of the minders interviewed, notably those who themselves had worked when their children were young and had used childminders.

The strength of the feelings held by both minders and mothers, which have been indicated above, point to the highly emotive nature of childminding as an activity. The employed mother who places her child in the care of a childminder is doing something which the minder would never do herself. The childminder, on the other hand, by remaining at home with her own children, is pursuing a course which the mother, either from choice or necessity, has decided against. This distinction is of fundamental importance to the way in which minders and mothers perceive each other's role, and is likely to be a key factor in the way in which relationships develop within the childminding situation.

The issue was addressed, albeit in a somewhat indirect way, on the pre-registration courses which we observed in the two study areas. In both cases, the tutors raised the subject of parents' needs, wishes and expectations in seeking day care. In Waltham Forest, explicit reference was made to the tensions experienced by employed mothers, in the context of a discussion about whether or not minders should look after sick children (they are not obliged to do so). One coordinator pointed out that taking time off work was often difficult for women with young children, who could thereby suffer discrimination by employers.

What was particularly revealing from our observations of the courses was that, in both areas, individual participants expressed, implicitly or explicitly, the critical views of employed mothers which we have quoted above. In Bracknell, a group exercise to consider what a parent might be looking for in a childminder revealed that many course participants did not understand how a mother *could* leave her child in the care of someone else and would certainly not be prepared to do this themselves. In Waltham Forest, group members expressed the view that parents looked upon work as 'relaxation time', and found childcare irksome. One participant observed that mothers wanted to go shopping without their children, but since she had managed to combine the two, she saw no reason why others could or should not.

In all of the above examples, the implications of such views for the relationship between childminder and mother are considerable, but were not explored in any great depth by the trainers. Although, as noted in the previous chapter, Waltham Forest coordinators would follow-up specific issues of concern with individual applicants, it does seem important that salient attitudes to childminders are fully addressed within courses such as these.

Parents' day care preferences

Before moving on to look at how our sample childminding arrangements came about, it is important to consider what the parents concerned were actually seeking in their day care placements, including, of course, whether childminding was their preferred form of provision. A number of studies have indicated that childminding is less popular with parents than nursery or group care, and that for many users it represents very much a second best (for example, Bone, 1977). Our own investigation presented a rather different picture, with just over half (17) of the parents expressing a preference for childminding over other forms of provision, whether actually available to them or not.

It is likely that this finding reflected the age distribution of the children concerned; indeed several parents specifically mentioned that they considered childminding most appropriate for babies or toddlers. Favoured alternatives to childminding included a live-in or day nanny, day nursery (local authority or private), workplace nursery and nursery school.

Although the sample was small and not necessarily representative, it is worth noting that only four families expressed a preference for workplace nurseries. This is especially significant in view of the publicity and attention currently given to workplace provision as a solution to the unmet need for day care.

The reasons given by those for whom childminding was first choice invariably centred on the family setting in which it was provided and its potential for individual attention and a warm relationship with one caring adult. For these parents, childminding was seen as more 'natural' and informal, and valued as the nearest approximation to the family home. One mother, herself a teacher, claimed that she was:

'not that keen on them going to a formal sort of nursery too early... I just thought it would be more natural for her to go to a childminder – being with a family. As if she was just round at a friend's house, you know... and she'd do all the things that I'd do with her if I was at home.'

The importance of a home environment and personal care was stressed particularly by parents of babies and younger children; indeed, as we have noted, the preference for childminding was most marked among those whose children were in the lower half of the pre-school age range.

'I think it is better for babies and children up to... maybe one and a half, two, if they are with a childminder... they're sort of in somebody's *home* – they're looked after one-to-one.'

'I was going to get a childminder or I wasn't going back to work... because I think it's best to have a one-to-one relationship for the child rather than be stuck with a lot of children. I think if you can't be there, the next best thing is to find somebody that's going to care about them, and put them in a home environment.'

Despite the frequent use of the term 'one-to-one', only one parent actually stated that she was seeking a day care setting in which her son would be alone with a childminder. The presence of at least a *small* number of other children was also seen as a desirable feature amongst those who opted for childminding. Two families who had considered, but rejected, the possibility of a nanny, saw childminding as a positive transitional setting between home and group situations.

'We had thought about a (day nanny) but we plumped for a childminder... we thought it would give her more stimulation and be more interesting... it would be really boring for (child) to be stuck at home.'

The reasons which parents gave for preferring childminding to other day care options were almost exclusively centred on the perceived interests of their children. The only expressed advantage to the parents themselves was the flexibility of timing offered by childminding as opposed to group care, but this was an important consideration to those whose work involved unsocial or irregular hours.

'A lot of nurseries were too inflexible for my needs... if I finish early I want to pick him up – most nurseries found that to be a problem.'

'A nursery wouldn't give me any flexibility. When we started with (childminder) there was a possibility that I would be going to some evening meetings lasting till 10 p.m. and (father) wouldn't always be there to pick her up.'

Parents who would have preferred a day nursery place also gave child-centred reasons for their views; but, in contrast to the home environment and close relationships sought by those opting for childminding, these parents were more concerned to place their children in what they saw as a structured, stimulating environment, where they would mix with a group of other children, under the care of qualified staff.

'I think there are probably more opportunities for them in a nursery. The staff are more trained if you like. The day is probably far better structured than it is in a normal house... I would like her to have the sort of environment that is a little more stimulating than I imagine the home situation would be.'

'Well... I mean, they're *professionals* in their own right and I think that's the best place for kids to get the *grounding*... you know, when they're starting life... A day nursery is about trying... not to educate them as such, but being more aware of their physical and mental needs at that age.'

There is clearly an important contrast here in what parents were seeking from day care; between those who wanted it to reproduce as far as possible the routines and relationships of the family setting, and those who looked to day care to provide experiences which home could not offer anyway. Interestingly, the few parents who expressed a preference for a workplace nursery revealed a different perspective again; giving reasons for their choice which indicated their own desire to retain proximity to their children. For example, one father, whose work was located much closer to home than his wife's, said:

'If we had a free choice I would very much like a crèche system at work... It would be quite pleasant to know I can go to work with my little girl... I can leave her with the nurse and pop in and see her at breaktime... have lunch together in the staff canteen... that everything is on tap if I need to see her.'

Implicit in the above comments is the parents' wish to spend as much time as possible with their children and to remain in charge of their care. Interestingly, one of the perceived attractions of a nanny to those who stated this as their first choice, was the sense of *control* which this enabled parents to retain, as the following interview extract illustrates.

Father: 'I would have gone for a nanny if money was no object... We would have felt she would probably have been in the house...

Mother: Yes... I would have felt more in control...

Father: The nanny's totally employed to look after the child... I think we'd insist more... that the nanny spent so much time reading or doing certain things... whereas if you go to a childminder you tend to feel you have to leave it more up to her.'

It is important to note here how the varied reasons given for preferring one or other form of day care – even when expressed solely in terms of perceived benefits to children – allude to the highly emotive, and often ambivalent, feelings which day care can arouse in parents. This was demonstrated most vividly in the following comments of a mother who had voiced a strong preference for nursery provision:

'In an institution like a school or nursery it's easier because there's a sort of understanding that that's what they're there for... It's not natural to sort of give your child to another person in their home – it's more natural to take them to a school or nursery and leave them. I think you feel... well, *safer*... I'd feel more at ease.'

Such feelings are likely to play a powerful part in influencing how parents approach childminders and negotiate their arrangements. Before turning to what actually happened at this point in our case studies, however, we look at how the parents and childminders in the sample actually came into contact with one another. In particular, we focus on the public dimension to this stage of arranging day care, in terms of the part played by social services workers.

Linking parents with childminders

From our interviews with the childminding advisers and coordinators in the two study areas, it appeared that policy and practice with regard to linking parents and prospective childminders was rather different. In Waltham Forest, the aim was to provide a more substantive service to parents by interviewing them in order to identify their day care preferences, and then to offer the names of childminders who appeared to meet their requirements. In both areas, however, parents were encouraged to visit and consider several possible minders before making their own informed choice. Nonetheless, the accounts given by the parents in both locations suggested that, for them, the reality of selecting a childminder was not the planned, rational process which this might suggest. Only 11 of the 30 had visited more than one potential provider and, for many, finding a suitable placement had been a nerve-racking experience.

Most (two out of three) had begun their search by approaching their local social services department. (The remainder either already knew the person who was to become their childminder, or had been recommended to her by a friend or previous minder.) For those who had gone through official channels in Bracknell, the subsequent receipt of an unedited list of registered childminders had, in many cases, meant a time-consuming and frustrating experience. One mother had solicited the help of teacher colleagues in sifting through 'a huge list – you don't know if they're full or not – it's not kept up to date'. Another couple had found the information similarly unhelpful:

Mother: 'I managed to get hold of the list eventually, but it didn't have any telephone numbers on.'
Father: 'You've got to keep phoning Directory Enquiries to get phone numbers. To me that's just crazy. (Then) you've got to find out who has a vacancy. I think they're pretty supportive of the childminders, but of the parents – I think the service is almost non-existent.'

The perceived lack of information and support available to would-be users of childminding was keenly felt and cogently expressed by one father in Bracknell.

'I think there should be some help in what to expect... I think social services... should be supporting you, otherwise you're on your own... The crucial thing is information... I don't see why they can't supply us with a short CV. And if social services *do* go round and check, we should have access to that information.'

As we saw in Chapter 4, a more interventionist role in initiating day care arrangements was adopted by the social services department in Waltham Forest. For most of the parents in the study, the interview with a childminding coordinator and her subsequent assistance in finding a childminder had been highly valued. As one mother explained:

'I had an interview with (coordinator) – she didn't bother putting me in touch with people she knew wouldn't be suitable. If she thought somebody *was* suitable, she would phone them up first to see if they were available.'

However, the experience of one or two Waltham Forest parents suggested that the social services' contribution was not always considered helpful.

'Basically it's just like somebody reeling off a list of names in *Yellow Pages* – "Yeah – these are the people with vacancies". You get the impression that if that is all their involvement... it seems a very loose control over the system.'

Other factors also appeared to influence social services' effectiveness in assisting parents. *Time* played a crucial part in the process, in a way which created pressure and stress, and prevented the careful planning of day care arrangements which many parents – especially those with new babies – had tried to achieve. Mothers on maternity leave began seeking day care well ahead of their return to work – in one case even before the baby's birth. But, due to uncertainty about which minder would have vacancies, social services workers would not, or could not, initiate the process until nearer the required date. As one mother put it:

'They don't do a list in this part of Waltham Forest – they act like some kind of dating agency! And they will only interview you about six weeks before you start work, so you have to exaggerate why you need longer... They have a tendency to come up with someone at the last minute.'

In some cases, however, even such eleventh-hour moves did not produce a satisfactory outcome:

'It was a matter of a few weeks before I actually went back to work – she started phoning and saying "Somebody has come up, would you like to go and see them?" In the end we hadn't found anybody suitable...It was a case of "we have got to find somebody – will we have that person or stick out for somebody we really want?"... My sister came and stayed for three weeks and she had him... I don't know what we'd have done if she hadn't.'

Even more stressful was the situation of parents whose previous childminding arrangement had terminated – usually at short notice – and who urgently needed to find a suitable alternative. In such cases, the inability of social services to respond effectively to parental needs was particularly evident.

'(Coordinator) gave me the names of two people. I phoned one – she hadn't got a place any more. The other one I went round to and she said it had just been taken.'

This situation could create considerable difficulties for parents, as illustrated by the experience of the following couple, who had removed their daughter from an unsatisfactory placement and were desperate to find a quick solution to their problem. The mother telephoned social services, where only a clerical assistant was available.

'I said "Have you got any childminders?" and she said "No – what about nurseries?" I said "Well, I've tried, but she doesn't come within the three categories." And she said "What about private?" I said "I've tried that... She's got to be potty trained." And she said "Well, have you thought about giving up work for a little while?" And I thought, "well! that's not quite the solution I was looking for!"'

In seeking to help parents find a suitable childminder, social services workers are clearly hampered by the constraints of the context within which childminding operates and the resources available to them. In Waltham Forest, for example, the inadequate supply of child-minders, referred to earlier by the coordinators, meant that the chance that parents could be offered several possibilities was severely reduced, and the aimed-for 'matching service' became wishful thinking. It was also evident that, in both Waltham Forest and Bracknell, social services departments, with their existing staff resources, were unable to keep abreast of the supply situation while undertaking their other duties, such as registration and the associ-ated tasks. Our earlier research showed that relatively few minders routinely inform the department when a vacancy occurs (Ferri and Birchall, 1987). In such circumstances, therefore, it is unlikely that childminding workers, even if they wished, could offer parents the support desired by one father in Waltham Forest who commented that he was:

'vaguely surprised that the broking role of the childminding coordinator seemed to be limited... I feel perhaps there could have been a more obvious role, saying "Let's have a meeting (with a childminder) – I will be there too", or "Pop along to my office – I will arrange to have a couple of childminders here and we can have a chat" '.

It is also pertinent to note that, in the essentially private framework in which childminding takes place, there is no regulatory obligation on providers to make their services equally accessible to all potential users. In view of this, it was important to consider whether and how this issue was addressed by the childminder training initiatives in the two areas. From our observation of the pre-registration courses, it appeared that the messages being conveyed to applicants were somewhat ambiguous. On the one hand, they were urged to be responsive to parents' needs and wishes in deciding whether to accept a placement, while on the other, emphasis was laid on taking account of their own and their families' interests in delineating the boundaries of their services. In Waltham Forest, for example, course participants were advised to decide for themselves what was legitimately to be considered as childminding work: '*You* need to decide what's reasonable – where your job *stops*.' This approach serves to underline the structural isolation in which private child-minders undertake their work; in particular the lack of a supportive framework of employment and the consequent need to construct their own job descriptions.

The findings from our case studies indicated that childminders do indeed impose certain restrictions which enable their caring activity to blend compatibly with the domestic context in which it is provided. As their motives for childminding suggest, the perceived needs of their own families are paramount in childminders' approach to their work. As two of our sample members put it:

'I wouldn't do minding if it didn't suit the family – if the kids hated it.'

'I would give up if it interfered with the family – obviously your family's got to come first before anybody else's family.'

One of the main areas in which minders exercised discretion in accepting placements was the *age* of the child to be minded. Many parents in the study had experienced difficulty in finding someone who would take a young baby, although one or two childminders actually expressed a *preference* for babies. Significantly, perhaps, this was explained in terms of the ease with which a baby could be 'moulded' to fit in with the minder's own domestic regime, especially as it concerned her own children – a topic to which we shall return later. Generally, the age of the child to be minded in relation to those of the minder's own family was an important consideration; one minder would only take pre-school children since her own sons were at junior school, and to accept older minded children would, she felt, 'undermine their authority'.

Another major factor in this context was *time*. Several child-minders in the sample preferred – or even restricted their services to – teachers' children, in order to have school holidays free to devote to their own families. In terms of daily routine, childminders' commitments to accompanying their own children to and from school placed constraints upon the times they were available to receive minded children or their parents.

Finally, one childminder in the study who was, of course, registered with the social services department, stated that she would only agree to care for a child of someone she knew; a situation which our earlier research suggested was far from uncommon, since many people become registered only to legalise an existing arrangement with a friend (Ferri and Birchall, 1987).

Seen from the childminder's perspective, setting such boundaries around the service offered is understandable and reasonable. Looked at as the major day care service for working parents, however, it is clear that doing so can produce serious restrictions in terms of availability of provision and equality of access.

Having pointed out the ways in which many childminders set limits upon the services they offered, it also needs to be noted that, *within* these boundaries, they showed considerable flexibility in meeting the day care needs of parents. As Table 5.5 indicates, the number of days and hours for which care was provided varied widely, reflecting the childminders' responsiveness to the particular circumstances and requests of individual parents.

Table 5.5 Details of care arrangements in sample cases

	Number
5 days, full day (8 hours or more)	16
less than 5 days, full day	5
5 days, part-time	1
less than 5 days, part-time	4
varying each week	4
Total	30

It is important to note that in only half of the sample cases was full day care provided for five days a week. This illustrates not only the great variety of day care needs among employed parents, but also the fact that, in responding to those needs, many childminders forfeit the opportunity to maximise their earnings. This is a significant point in relation to the economics of this type of day care, a topic which we shall examine more closely in the next chapter.

First contacts between parents and childminders

'I wanted to find a person I could relate to and entrust my baby to. It was as simple and as difficult as that.'

In the preceding section we referred to a childminder who would only offer her services to someone she already knew. Such sentiments were not exclusive to providers, however. One of the mothers in the study who had placed her child in the care of a friend would not have considered anyone else and 'would dread having to find another minder and go through the proper channels'.

Such views, while by no means typical, are important in implicitly pointing to one of the most paradoxical and discomforting aspects of most childminding situations – the coming together of *strangers* to form an arrangement which, by its very nature, involves *intimate* relationships, locating the care of a child from one family within the private domestic setting of another.

The parents' views

The effects of this incongruity were vividly illustrated in the accounts given of the first encounters between the parents and minders in our study. Typically, these involved one or both parents visiting the minder in her house to discuss their requirements and her provision. For many parents the situation was fraught with apprehension about entrusting the care of their child to someone they did not know. One young couple described their feelings about the first meeting with their prospective minder:

Father: 'I was very nervous.'
Mother: 'Yes, it was a bit frightening. You're leaving them eight hours a day with somebody else. I feel... I sort of *abandoned* her to this stranger who wouldn't know all her little quirks and funny ways. It was very daunting.'

Despite – or perhaps, in some ways, because of – the momentous nature of the subject of the first encounter, the most typical feelings recalled in most parents' accounts of the meetings were of inhibition. Even those who had carefully planned their approach by reading advice books, consulting experienced friends, and preparing lists of questions on topics of importance, found themselves unable to pursue their strategy.

Mother: 'I went with a whole list of questions, and when we got there we didn't actually ask any of the questions.'
Father: 'We felt very embarrassed to ask.'

The general discomfort experienced by parents in this situation was emphasised by a mother who, as a social worker, was obviously accustomed to conducting interviews and assessments. When asked how she had felt about the initial meeting with her childminder she replied:

'Awful – I hated it! They know you are sizing them up and I think they are sizing you up – it's not a very pleasant feeling to be quite honest.'

The constraints felt by parents in asking what another mother described as 'all these hard-hitting questions' would seem to be largely rooted in the strong perception of the childminder's home and family life as an essentially *private* domain and hence not a legitimate area for what would be seen as intrusive questioning. This presents a major dilemma for parents who found it difficult, if not impossible, to obtain what was for them crucial information about the family setting to which they might entrust their child.

Mother: 'It is (difficult) when you've only just met. I suppose you shy away from asking the obvious on the first meeting, don't you?'

Father: 'Because you might be out of line asking those sorts of questions...'

And, as another mother put it:

'It was a nerve-racking experience, actually, going into somebody else's home to interview them. It just didn't seem right!'

The perceived territorial prerogative of childminders extended to parents' reluctance to probe too deeply into childminders' views and values regarding childcare, or to be what they clearly considered as over-assertive in explicitly stating their own position and what was important to them in the day care treatment of their children. One mother, when asked if the issue of discipline had been discussed at the initial meeting, replied:

'We tended to skirt round that area... you don't like to say, "Well I'm a hard disciplinarian" when the person in front of you says, "Well, no, I allow him to do exactly as he likes." '

Another mother felt that the power balance in respect of what was to take place in the day care setting clearly favoured the childminder.

'I don't think you can be that fussy, because if you're leaving your child in somebody's house then they're going to have to conform to their sort of standards and beliefs about bringing up children... I think you've usually got to accept that.'

The only exceptions to this pattern were a small group of parents who held a contrasting perception of the power relationship between users and providers of day care. These parents saw themselves in the dominant role of employer, as illustrated by the following comments from a father: 'At the end of the day... you're paying the wages, so to a certain extent you can call the tune.'

In general, however, parents' feelings about the first meeting with a prospective childminder were characterised by inhibition. Such views were especially prevalent among those who felt themselves to be in a relatively powerless position in what they found to be a sellers' market. Far from feeling able to express their particular wishes, these parents sensed that they themselves were being interviewed and judged as to their acceptability as clients. One couple, whose previous arrangement had ended suddenly, described how:

Mother: 'We were a bit panicky...'
Father: 'I thought she was interviewing us basically... to see what sort of people we were... probably to see how easy her job would be looking after (child). She said what she wanted and we agreed.'

And another mother who found herself in a similar position felt that:

'it was like being interviewed about (child) – whether she was going to be good enough to go there.'

The childminders' views
Like an echo of the apprehension which most of the parents in the study had experienced over their first meeting with their childminders, it was clear from the providers' accounts that many of them, too, had approached the occasion with some trepidation. Whereas the parents had felt hesitant about intruding upon another's private domain, the minders experienced some discomfort in the feeling that they and their homes were the objects of scrutiny.

'I suppose I was a little bit nervous... they are coming into my home, and you look around and think – will he be all right here, is it clean enough for them and that type of thing... really judging you and the house.'

The sense of mutual discomfort which many childminders described was not conducive to an atmosphere in which pertinent information and views could be openly and easily exchanged. Experience did not necessarily lessen the difficulties, as one childminder of 15 years' practice described:

'I think the parents do get tense and the minder gets tense – I do anyway. When you meet a new person for the first time you don't actually know what to say to them, do you?'

As well as feeling themselves under judgement, however, childminders had their own assessments to make at the first encounter with potential customers. Given the importance they attached to the compatibility of childminding and family life, a major consideration was whether the new child would 'fit in'. As one minder explained when asked what she sought from the initial meeting: 'I wanted to see if (child) would get on with my daughter and myself'.

Childminders were also anxious, however, to gauge the extent to which the parents' expectations of the arrangement in terms of child-care would harmonise with their own established domestic scene.

'Sometimes you get mums who come in and *demand* – they want this for the child, they want that. You think well, they're going to be interfering all the time – you get the vibes that "I don't think they're going to settle down." '

A further source of anxiety for childminders was whether the parents who were seeking their services would prove reliable in terms of time-keeping and payment. Our own earlier investigation, as well as those of other researchers (for example, Moss, 1987), showed that such issues are by far the most common source of reported friction between childminders and parents, and several of the minders in the present study attributed their concern over these matters at the initial meeting to previous unhappy experiences.

'I have learned my lesson... 99 per cent of the parents I have had do not consider childminding as a job. I have had a parent owe me £100 and say, "Can't you borrow it from your husband – I'll give it to you tomorrow!" '

The issue of finance, and the difficulties it presents to both childminders and parents, is of major importance to the conduct of day care arrangements, and will be explored more fully in the next chapter, which focuses on the business aspect of childminding.

The agenda with which childminders approached their first meeting with new parents was thus a complex mixture of self-promotion and critical assessment. As one of the Bracknell minders put it when asked what she wanted from the encounter:

'Well, I suppose I wanted her to like me. I wanted to know exactly what she wanted. I didn't want to be played about with because you do get some mothers, you know – they're doing you a favour... They pick them up when they feel like it... You've got to really make your mind up, is this one going to be right for you?'

Exchanging information

In the foregoing accounts, we have drawn attention to the respective qualms of minders and parents which could make the initial contact and discussion between the two parties a difficult exercise, since it is with such issues that childminder training needs to be more deeply concerned. Despite varying degrees of discomfort and apprehension, however, many of the interviewees gave detailed accounts of wide-ranging discussions and exchange of information in arranging the day care placement. In general, these covered the broad areas of the practical details of hours and charges, the home experience and personal characteristics of the child to be minded, and the nature of the care that the childminder would provide, as the following extracts from the accounts of a mother and her childminder illustrate.

Mother: 'I wanted to know... a bit of her own family background, how she got involved with childminding, how long she'd been doing it... just get a feeling for the person... how many children does she have now... what her daily routine is like... to explain to her what my expectations were in the way of feeding (baby), changing nappies, going out, taking her to different places. Finding out if I had a problem at work, could I have an 'extension' at short notice, or how much notice did she like to feel comfortable.'

Minder: 'I wanted to know exactly how mum fed the baby. How she held her, whether or not she had a dummy... because sometimes they don't tell you and you've got this poor little mite thrust on you that you don't know... I tend to let her say what they expect of a childminder; then I say what I expect of a childminder, and take it from there.'

Another childminder described how, although she and the mother of her new placement already knew each other, she attached great importance to the detailed exchange of information regarding childcare practice: 'I discuss things right down to whether they use a knife and fork or a fork and spoon'.

Underlying these childminders' insistence upon eliciting information about children and how they were treated at home was a commitment to trying, as far as possible, to reproduce the family environment.

'I wanted to know if she had a certain time that she slept, a certain time she was fed – I wanted to keep her in the routine she was used to, so it didn't seem too much of a change for her.'

There were also, however, a few cases in which minder and parent did not appear to have exchanged much information about their respective approaches to childcare before the arrangement began. On the parents' side this seemed to reflect the inhibitions described earlier with regard to expressing their own wishes and seeking information about the childminder. Such parents appeared to make optimistic assumptions that all would be as they hoped. One mother, for example, after acknowledging that she did not want a minder who smoked, added:

'The trouble is I never ask. But looking at (minder) you just wouldn't imagine her to smoke or do anything wrong.'

The few childminders in this group appeared, for their part, to view the purpose of meeting with parents as to outline their own terms, conditions and childcare practice, in the expectation of compliance by those who agreed to place their children with them.

'I just say what I want to put over to them – my terms and that – if they don't like it they can go somewhere else. Because obviously they've got to fit in with what I do and how I brought up my children.'

Such examples were, however, a minority, and in most of our sample cases, a considerable amount of relevant information was exchanged regarding each side's approach to childcare.

Clearly, we cannot document in detail the varied and wide-ranging discussions which took place, or the precise areas in which minders and parents explicitly agreed to pursue one or the other's approach, reached a compromise, or left particular issues unaddressed or unresolved. But whether and how matters of concern to each party are discussed in creating the framework for a day care placement is obviously an important issue for childminder training.

In both Bracknell and Waltham Forest, the initial contact between childminders and parents was explicitly recognised as a key point in the day care arrangement, and was included in the pre-registration course curriculum in each area. As far as most of the minders in our study were concerned, however, the coverage appeared to have made little impact. Of the four who had attended the courses we observed, two made no reference to the subject, while one obliquely mentioned that discussion of 'the business side' had been useful. Only the fourth, who had welcomed the course because she 'didn't like the first visits and thought it would try to get me over them...' explicitly stated that she had found it helpful in this respect. Interestingly, however, she added that the '(trainers) were explaining the practical side of it, whereas the minders tell the emotional side of it'.

A couple of childminders who had attended earlier courses referred to sessions dealing with initial negotiations with parents and said that they had found them helpful in dealing with practicalities.

'I didn't have a clue – didn't know what to talk about. It's most important to know to ask the right questions – get everything ready for the contract.'

The recalled emphasis on being 'businesslike' suggests that the underlying emotive nature of childminding, as revealed implicitly or explicitly by both minders and parents in this study, is given insufficient recognition in training measures to help minders deal with setting up a day care arrangement. There would seem to be a need to focus greater attention on this aspect, and raise minders' awareness, not only of the feelings and motivations of parents seeking day care, but also of the values and beliefs which they themselves bring to the childminding situation.

It also seems important to stress that there can be no single formula for facilitating initial meetings. While some parents appreciated the businesslike approach which minders had been urged by trainers to adopt, others, as we have seen, rejected it as callous self-interest. It was ironic to find that one minder, pursuing the seemingly irreproachable advice given on the training course to create a relaxed atmosphere by offering refreshments, only increased the sense of inhibition experienced by the parents. As the mother pointed out:

'When somebody offers you a coffee, you don't produce a list of questions from your bag and say, "Right..." '

The experiences recalled by many of the parents in the study suggest that here, as in other areas we have mentioned, they too would benefit from some form of advice or counselling on seeking and negotiating day care. One father explicitly stated that:

'with hindsight, it would have been nice if social services had given us an idea of what we should have been looking for, how we should be going about it, the sort of things we should be asking.'

Judging whether to proceed

The crucial decision to be taken at the end of the initial meeting(s) between childminder and parent was whether or not to proceed with the placement. It is interesting to note at this point that the content of the early discussions between the two parties was largely factual – covering details of the child's eating and sleeping habits, and medical history, as well as the practical details of hours and charges. As we have seen, however, the crucial considerations on both sides were *emotional* and hinged on personal relationships as yet unestablished.

Consequently, neither the parents' anxiety to find someone to whom they could entrust their child, nor the minders' concern that the child would blend into her family setting and the parents prove reliable and untroublesome, were subject to rational assessment on the basis of one or two exploratory meetings.

On both sides, therefore, decisions were taken on the basis of intuitive feelings. As one minder put it: 'It's what you feel inside'. Terms such as 'instinct', and 'gut reaction' recurred again and again in parents' explanations of why they had settled for their particular minder.

'I just felt happy when I went in.'

Mother: 'I sort of clicked with her – you know, I just felt things were right.'
Father: 'I think it's more emotional... when you go round you decide on emotions rather than facts.'

In some cases, the fact that no explicit exchange of view had taken place was not considered important. As one father put it:

'You're sometimes not aware of things you're looking for... but you can imagine with that person... that they were safe. That their ideas were similar to yours. It's a certain amount of empathy between the people.'

There were, however, some more concrete pointers to what had contributed to parents' sense of confidence. The most frequently mentioned was the demeanour of the minder's own children.

Mother: '(Childminder) was very nice... but it wasn't that that made the decision, was it? It was as soon as we met (her daughter)...'
Father: 'That was definitely it... if she had two children like that...'

One mother, who knew her childminder already, felt that: 'The way she brought up her own gave me insight'. Another recalled the advice given by friends:

'A lot of people said, "Look at her kids – this is how yours will turn out, so if you like her kids you don't need to worry." '

Conversely, some parents made reference to other childminders whom they had rejected on account of the negative impression conveyed by their own children.

'You looked at her own children... and they were wild. I mean, she admitted that her older boy couldn't read very well.'

Whether positive or negative, such comments reveal the implicit perception on the part of parents regarding the childminder's role and influence; that is, that the relationship she has with minded children is comparable to that with her own, and that her influence on the two will be similar. In other words, the childminder's suitability as a day care provider was assessed in terms of her perceived success as a mother.

How minders reacted to their child at the first meeting also made a deep impression upon parents, although their views were highly personal and by no means consistent. Some warmed to those who immediately turned their attention to the child; others were less enthused by what they saw as 'taking over'. The sensitive atmosphere of the first encounter was depicted by one mother – a social worker – who said:

'I have got the baby with me – at what stage to hand over the baby and see how she is going to handle her? Much as I do this kind of thing in my job for other people, it's quite something else when it's you!'

However, parents were more united in their positive feelings about minders who displayed more interest in the child than in the business aspect of the arrangement.

'She was interested in him... what was he like?... what sort of things should she do to soothe him? I thought that was really great... How many people ask that? People were just jumping in telling me how much it was. The last thing we talked about was the money... She said we would speak about that later... "Go away and think about it." '

Again, numerous references were made to childminders who had been rejected on such grounds, for example:

'We did go to a couple of people and we took (child) along and they hardly looked at him! They were talking about terms and hours and things like that.'

Childminders also explained that intuitive judgement had played a large part in their decision regarding whether the child would 'fit in' with their family and other minding arrangements, and parents prove cooperative and reliable.

'The parent has to get on with us and vice versa; the child has to take to me and my children as well as we take to him. If there is a slight bit of tenseness or anything, I would say no.'

In cases where childminders knew the previous day care provider, their colleagues could often give them reassurance:

'(Other minder) said (mother) was a very nice person. She was trustworthy, she always came on time to collect (child); she was very good money-wise.'

All that helps to know that at the end of a week's work you're going to get paid for it and that mummy's going to turn up and collect the child.'

Contrasting concerns thus preoccupy parents and childminders as they try to assess the likelihood of a mutually satisfactory outcome. Also, the differing emotions and experiences which influence individual perspectives among both groups highlight the problematic nature of their first encounter. As a setting for negotiation, it is perhaps unique; concerned not only with factual matters, but with personal values and behaviour which inhabit the private province of family life, but which are fundamental to the main purpose of the meeting – provision for the care of a child.

The complexity and sensitivity of this issue points to the need, in many cases, for *both* parties to a childminding arrangement to receive help and support to become fully aware of what is crucial to them in the matter of day care, and of how they can discover and assess the values and behaviour of others. This is clearly a challenging yet vital task for childminder training and one which, according to our evidence, it has as yet barely begun to address.

The introductory process

To conclude our account of how the new childminding arrangements in the sample began, we move on to the actual start of the placements. The desirability of a gradual introduction to the day care setting, especially in the interests of the minded child, has generally received wide endorsement, and was advocated by those delivering the childminder training courses in our two study areas. Other researchers have expressed disquiet at their findings that, in many cases, settling-in visits were given insufficient consideration by minders and parents alike. Whether or not this occurs, however, is determined not only by the importance attached to it by both parties, but also by external circumstances.

In a number of our sample cases, the arrangement began with a series of introductory visits, involving mother and child together, or the child alone. Such procedures were agreed at the initial discussions, as in the case of the following example.

Mother: 'I was very keen to spend time with (minder), to get to know her a bit better… I wanted (child) to get the idea that it was all right for her to be with (minder), and that I was coming back and that it was consistently happening that way. I got the impression that (minder) was happier that I do that rather than come in on the day I'm going to work, leave the child and walk away.'

Childminder: 'Ideally it's the way it should be done. It was mutual... she said she wished to do it and I totally agreed with her.'

In other instances, however, introductory visits, either with or without the mother, were deemed unnecessary, since minder and parent and/or minder and child knew each other already. The latter example included children placed with a minder who knew their previous carer, either as a friend or through contact at a minders' group or drop-in-centre. In several cases involving very young babies, neither minder nor parent felt any need for 'settling' visits since the children, somewhat questionably perhaps, were considered too young to be aware of the situation.

For some, however, a gradual introduction to the day care setting would have been welcomed by the parents, but was precluded by the demands of their employment, or the pressure to find a childminder at short notice after a previous arrangement terminated. This situation was not always appreciated by childminders, however:

'Where it is going from one minder to another... sometimes they will just expect you to have the child on Monday morning because they won't want to take the time off work. We would prefer the child to have time to settle in rather than just dump them straightaway.'

It is also relevant to recall here that, in Waltham Forest, social services' suggestions regarding suitable minders were only offered shortly before the placement was required. This, too, could have a negative impact on the opportunity for a phased introduction. One mother, who had fewer such visits than she would have wished said:

'it would have been nice to do the classic thing of getting the baby used to the childminder, getting you used to the childminder, so you're confident and you know each other and it's not a big wrench for either... But the way they work the system, you can't do that.'

Closely linked to the practice of introductory visits, but also importantly different, is the notion of a 'trial period' at the start of an arrangement. Minders in both areas who had attended training courses referred to the recommendations to participants that a 'trial' of up to one month should be agreed at the outset.

'They suggested you do a trial basis – that way you don't commit yourself – they don't commit themselves and you can see how you get on with the child.'

'That is what you learn at the course – the first month is a trial really, for both of you.'

The notion of a trial period gives tacit recognition to the tentative nature of the arrangement agreed by childminder and parent. It also highlights the contrast between childminding and nursery care, in its implicit acknowledgement that the former is dependent for its success upon the personal compatibility of those involved. If this proves not to be the case, there is no scope for displacement or dissipation of the problem as there would be in a group care situation. The likely outcome, therefore, is that the arrangement will be terminated, and, for parents, the search for day care will begin again.

Conclusion

The impression which emerges from the preceding pages is that starting a childminding arrangement involves a strong element of risk. The main reason for this lies in the difficulty of forming rational judgements in advance concerning the complex areas of personal behaviour and values which are crucial to its success. An informed awareness regarding shared beliefs and practices in aspects of childcare which are of importance to each party can only be acquired gradually, as relationships develop. The difficult situation which this represents for childminders, and even more for parents, in nego-tiating a day care placement is heightened by the emotionally-charged context, which involves one side entrusting the care of a small child to the other.

This would seem to represent a key issue for training initiatives in the field of childminding. From what we have seen of training in our two study areas, however, it appears that current approaches barely scratch the surface of the emotive layer which is so important in this day care setting. Indeed, it could be argued that they give some reinforcement to certain contradictions inherent in the way child-minding at present operates.

The training objectives of the social services departments, as we saw implemented in the courses observed, were to encourage childminders to look upon their work as a professional service, responsive to the needs and wishes of potential clients. At the same time, however, the course presenters stressed the importance for would-be childminders, as home-based mothers, to consider the impact which caring for other people's children would have upon their own children, partners and family life. It is clear from what we have seen that these dual considerations may be in conflict; the needs and expectations emanating from the respective worlds of families seeking day care, and of those who provide it, do not necessarily coincide. It is vital that training measures enable childminders to become more fully aware of their own fundamental values and behaviour in matters of childcare and of the implications of these for undertaking the care of someone else's child.

Our findings have also indicated that many *parents* need, and would explicitly welcome, similar support in dealing with the conflicting emotions surrounding their decision to use day care; in considering what is important to them in terms of provision and in actually identifying and arranging an appropriate placement. It should not be forgotten, however, that the roots of many of the problems highlighted in this chapter lie in the essentially private structure within which childminding currently operates and which requires that the parties involved, especially parents, address these complex issues largely on their own.

6. The business of childminding

'I don't like asking people for money, if my husband was earning enough I wouldn't need the money. I think I would have all the children without being paid.' (Bracknell childminder)

A consistent theme in current training initiatives in the field of childminding encourages providers to view their work as an occupation, requiring an appropriately businesslike approach, as opposed to the informal, good neighbourly activity in which lie its historical roots. The underlying rationale among those involved in training, in both public authorities and grassroots organisations, is that childminding arrangements based on formally-agreed terms and conditions will advance the interests of *all* concerned, by contributing to a better quality service for both users and providers, and enhancing the status of childminders and their work.

The view of childminding as a *job* was thus strongly promulgated by those delivering the pre-registration courses in our two study areas. In the words of one of the day care advisers:

'You mustn't ever forget that you have chosen to do this as your job. The parents go to work to earn money – you're doing your work at home.'

Since, however, childminding takes place within a private market framework, the broad objectives of this branch of training was to equip childminders *themselves* to conduct their arrangements in a businesslike manner. Although, as we saw in the preceding chapter, social services workers played an important role in bringing childminders and parents into contact with one another, they had little or no involvement in setting the terms and conditions of a placement, or in its subsequent operation. One day care adviser in Bracknell referred during a training session to her standard reply to parents who enquired what childminders were supposed to charge: 'I say, "It's up to them – they can charge what they like." '

In similar vein, the detachment of the social services department from the day-to-day conduct of established childminding arrangements was illustrated by the response of the same worker to childminders who experienced difficulties over parental non-payment: 'All we can say is – it's your problem – it's up to you to sort out the money'.

Training efforts to inculcate businesslike attitudes and practices in the providers of home-based day care were included as part of the coverage of the final session of the pre-registration course in each area. Only a brief amount of time was thus available to offer advice and information on a wide range of complex topics, including the recommended use of contracts to formalise the various terms and conditions of the day care arrangements; the importance of insurance cover; and the relationship between income from childminding, and the systems of taxation and benefits. Greater detail was contained in the numerous leaflets and guidelines distributed to course participants. These included a range of publications from the National Childminding Association, one of which (an extract from a training pack produced in conjunction with The Open University) was entitled 'Turning it into a job'. This served to reinforce the occupational view of childminding which this part of the training course sought to promote.

In examining the impact of training in this area of childminding, our interest focused on how the advocacy of a businesslike approach blended with other perspectives which both childminders and parents might bring to the situation. In order to explore this issue in the necessary depth, we concentrated on two key aspects of the business aspect of childminding: first, the use of contracts to formalise the agreement and, secondly, how the subject of finance was dealt with by those involved in our 30 sample cases.

The use of contracts in childminding arrangements

The course presenters in both areas laid stress on the importance of employing a contract to record the agreed terms and conditions of each new day care arrangement. In both cases it was explained to participants that the contract was a legal document which could be used to support action to recover outstanding payments. One

Waltham Forest coordinator referred to the social services department's current support of a childminder who was pursuing payment of £170 through the Small Claims Court from a parent who had failed to give the agreed month's notice before removing her child.

Specimen forms of the type adopted in each area were distributed to course members. In Bracknell, the contract form was produced by the day care advisers and based on NCMA guidelines, while in Waltham Forest a rather more detailed document was the result of recent joint work by the social services department and the local childminding association, and carried their respective logos. One of the childminding coordinators in the London borough urged course participants to use the form as a basis for discussion with prospective customers: 'Have the paper in front of you... parents don't resent it so much' – a significant statement which tacitly recognises the potential for tension in the one-to-one negotiations between users and providers, as well as the power of a collective or public framework to alleviate it.

From the interviews carried out shortly after each arrangement began, it emerged that all but four (two in each area) of the 30 childminders involved had completed a contract which formalised the details of the agreement. Three of the four explained that they had run out of forms, while the other confessed to being 'a bit lax about that I'm afraid'. Although we clearly cannot draw conclusions about the direct influence of training in this respect, it is worth noting that three of the four were among the small group of eight childminders in the study who had *not* attended any courses.

The prevailing view expressed by both childminders and parents (about two-thirds in each case) was that the contract was a valuable method of clarifying and formalising the terms of the arrangement at the outset, and thereby avoiding subsequent confusion or conflict. One Bracknell minder, who had attended the course we observed, claimed that it had changed her whole approach:

'I would never really have thought of using a contract until I actually heard there was one... there are things on there that I wouldn't even have thought of – like if the parents are sick. I wouldn't know what to do in that situation, whereas in here it tells you.'

A colleague in the same area who had attended an earlier course recalled learning how:

'Some people have problems with payment. If you have it down in black and white, if need be, you can take it to the small claims department.'

In Waltham Forest, too, one of the participants on the observed pre-registration course expressed a feeling of reassurance that childminding arrangements were covered by written contracts:

'I felt better for it ... you've each got a copy and you can see what you've agreed to'.

Interestingly, another Waltham Forest childminder, who had never attended a course, had not used a contract when accepting her first placement and felt that she had learned a lesson:

'They used to pay whenever they had the money. She would turn up late – when I had been waiting an hour – then she wouldn't pay me for that hour. It was just a mess really. I think we needed the contract.'

As mentioned above, the majority of the parents in the study felt equally reassured that there was a formal structure to their day care arrangement. One Bracknell mother explained that she:

'would rather there was something written down ... for security on both sides. The thing that concerns me about childminding in general is it's very sort of "iffy" and up in the air.'

At the time of the first interview, another Bracknell mother was able to describe how the contract had already proved its worth in resolving a potential disagreement:

'It's absolutely essential because it's very difficult to remember what you've actually agreed. I made a mistake one week about payment and (minder) had to remind me about the agreement. I had actually worked it out wrong... that was why it was excellent to go back to something that was written.'

It was also interesting to discover that two sets of parents in Waltham Forest were not only surprised and impressed when their child-minder produced a formal contract, but also expressed the view that this conferred a heightened status on the activity of childminding.

'I didn't realise they were so organised. Having a contract made it much more like a job. I didn't think of it that way until I realised there was a contract, then it made me change my perception of it.'

Such comments as these suggest that the formal approach to the establishment of day care arrangements, which was advocated on the training courses, had been eagerly accepted and valued by both parties. However, not all of those involved in our sample cases attached such importance to the use of contracts, or perceived them as mutually beneficial safeguards. One small group of childminders (four) expressed criticism of their content and scepticism as to their effectiveness in cases of dispute.

'It's a good idea about the contract, (but) at the same time I have got done out of an awful lot of money... parents have gone on holiday, said they'll pay you when they come back... (then) they don't give a child back. I know there is a small court or something, but it is a lot of hassle and aggravation... I think on the contract we should really be protected more... where maybe (coordinator) can claim and say, "You owe so-and-so two weeks' money." '

'They sign the contract (but) they just don't turn up. The contract... it's not really worth writing one out really because you couldn't get your money back you know.'

It is, perhaps, significant that all the minders who expressed such views not only recounted the problems they had experienced with previous arrangements, but also belonged to that half of our sample who said that their earnings from childminding represented an essential part of their family income. It was not possible to unravel whether or not such events and circumstances had influenced their approach to formalising the arrangements we were studying. What is noteworthy, however, is that in three of the four cases in which minders expressed scepticism about contracts, the parents also appeared uncertain of its value or significance. One referred to it merely as a form for recording relevant phone numbers, and two others described it as a document weighted in favour of childminders rather than providing mutual protection. In the words of one father:

'It's protecting *her* rights... she's laying down *her* guidelines, *her* law. One thing I don't like about (minder) – probably all childminders – is that we really have very little say in anything... they are the powerful people.'

This particular case had brought together a minder who described difficulties with parents in the past, and a couple who, having removed their child from what they considered an unsatisfactory childminding arrangement, were under pressure to find an alternative placement quickly, in what they saw as a seller's market. These respective contexts seemed to have contributed to a sense of mutual caution (if not suspicion) and powerlessness which, as we shall see, did not bode well for the future success of the arrangement.

The perception of the contract as a 'minders's charter', as another father put it, was accepted with much more equanimity by parents who clearly felt less vulnerable. One mother, whose partner was a lawyer, referred cheerfully to his view that the contract was 'completely one-sided and geared for the childminder. But they do *need* protection'.

In marked contrast to the adversarial view of the contractual relationship, was that of another small group of childminders, whose apparent insouciance about the use of contracts was rooted in the feeling that such formality was unnecessary, even distasteful. The underlying attitude here ran counter to the notion of childminding as an occupation requiring an official framework. As one minder put it: 'I don't use the word contract – to me it's too *businesslike*'. In this case, the disinclination to adopt a formal approach to the day care arrangement was echoed by the parents, who, commenting on the importance they attached to the friendly, informal relationship with their childminder, added:

Father: 'In that respect I'm glad a contract wasn't signed like that – formalising it.'

Mother: 'Yes, it's not a commercial relationship – it's on the basis of "You and me, let's sort it out." '

The way in which the participants in the study felt about the commercial aspect of childminding, and in particular what was seen as its uncomfortable juxtaposition with other aspects of the day care arrangement, will be examined more closely in the next section, when we look at the financial side of the agreements. But it is worth noting here that the nature of the relationship between childminder and parent could clearly affect the way in which they approached the contractual issue, especially when the two parties were already friends or acquaintances. Where this was the case, formal agreements were likely to be considered unnecessary. One Bracknell childminder, who had attended the observed pre-registration course and whose first placement had been the child of a friend, dismissed the relevance of a contract.

'I don't think I would ever end up taking someone to court – especially a next door neighbour. I can see the need if it's someone you don't know.'

Although a contract form had actually been completed, the mother in this case also attached little importance to it, referring to it merely as an 'information sheet'.

Our earlier research, involving a survey of 200 childminders, found that a fifth of them knew the parents of their minded children prior to the placement, and a further quarter of the arrangements came about via mutual friends. If training courses are to instil in childminders a commitment to a businesslike approach, they will have to take account of this strong counteracting influence inherent in the way in which a high proportion of arrangements come into being. It also needs to be conveyed to prospective providers that formal agreements may be especially important in cases where care arrangements are based on assumptions linked to personal friendship, which may result in quite unanticipated conflict.

Finally, the pre-registration courses in each of our study areas also emphasised the importance of *updating* contracts. In Waltham Forest in particular, childminders were urged to review their arrangements at regular intervals of six months or a year, and, in the words of one of the coordinators, 'use the contract as a basis for change'. From our follow-up interviews, however, there was little evidence that this was the practice. Despite numerous changes in times of attendance and charges, in only one sample case had the contract been reviewed and amended. It seemed, then, that the contracts were regarded, by most childminders and parents, as an important element in *setting the framework* for an arrangement. In the words of one of the fathers in the study:

'You've got to have that structure, you've got to have that contract, otherwise it makes it difficult... Can we do this? Can we do that? What happens if this happens? You feel as if you've got... some basis to it. You don't feel as if you're in it on your own... But then, when it comes down to it, you can remove that bit of paper and the whole thing would work anyway... what actually happens is we just get on with it.'

For some, however, other factors ran counter to the formality of contractual agreement even at the outset, and, as we shall see, these assumed greater significance as the arrangement continued. As one of the Bracknell childminders explained:

'I think you have to get the business side of it out of the way. When (arrangement) changed, I said to her perhaps we should sit down and decide (terms). But then it was quite difficult to talk to her about it because...she's become a friend.'

The financial aspect of childminding

The conflicting forces acting to determine whether or not childminding was regarded by those involved as a business became more clearly evident when we turned our attention to the issue of finance. One feature of the private framework in which most childminding takes place is that the question of payment for the care provided is a matter for individual childminders and parents to agree between them. The only exception to this involves cases in which a child's or family's need for day care meets the priority criteria for admission to local authority day nurseries. Where such provision is insufficient (or, as in Bracknell, non-existent), or childminding is considered to be a preferable alternative, social services departments are empowered to pay all or part of a childminder's fees. Bracknell, in fact, employed one salaried childminder to meet the needs of families eligible for publicly-funded day care, while Waltham Forest operated a much more extensive scheme for parents who qualified for financial assistance with day care costs.

In both areas, however, as elsewhere, private financial agreements were the norm, and this was the context to which those presenting the pre-registration courses applied their information and advice. It was explained to applicants that it was up to each one of them to set their own scale of charges. At the same time, however, they were urged to practice discretion when considering the circumstances of individual families such as lone parents, *and* also to adhere to the local pay guidelines – in order, as an experienced minder tutoring the Bracknell course explained, to avoid situations in which parents moved children around in pursuit of cheaper rates. Prospective childminders were thus presented with three potentially competing reference points when considering what to charge: their own personal aspirations, the collective interests of a peer group, and the individual circumstances of the consumer. The unambiguous message transmitted, however, was that it was up to each one of them to reconcile these.

The problem with money

The topic of money has been well documented as one of the most sensitive issues in the area of private childminding. It has been highlighted as a common cause of friction between childminders and parents, and of the acrimonious termination of arrangements (for example, Bryant and others, 1980; Mayall and Petrie, 1979). The widespread antipathy with which childminders regard the subject was acknowledged by the presenters of the pre-registration courses. As one Bracknell day care advisor put it:

'It's very hard to talk about money, isn't it? You've really *got* to be businesslike.'

In a later reference to the opportunities afforded by the Enterprise Allowance Scheme, the same advisor commented:

'This is all the frightening side of it isn't it? You don't think of all this as appertaining to childminding!'

These projected sentiments were, in fact, a fairly accurate reflection of the feelings of the childminders – and, for that matter, the parents – in our study. Almost everyone we interviewed indicated a deep aversion, not only talking about financial issues, but also to the subsequent transactions themselves. As one childminder put it:

'The thing I don't like discussing is money. I feel – what if she doesn't agree, or thinks it's too much? I think most minders say they hate discussing money.'

And, in the words of a mother in the study:

'I didn't like discussing it really; and I didn't even like paying her the first few weeks. It was really embarrassing.'

While the training sessions we observed gave explicit recognition to these negative feelings, the more deeply-rooted issue of *why* it should be so difficult or 'frightening' to deal with matters of finance was not explored. Yet this has major implications for the relationships between providers and users of childminding, and it is essential to analyse the situation more closely – not only in order to understand what actually takes place in a private childminding situation, but also, importantly, to evaluate the contribution of a training strategy which advocates a more businesslike approach as the solution to the problem.

Before turning to our study's findings in this area, however, it is useful to put them into context by looking at the actual financial framework surrounding the 30 sample cases; in particular, the basic charges for day care and how far these reflected the 'going rate' in each locality.

The cost of childcare

At the time of our initial interviews, the 'going rate' for childminding was the same in both areas; £1 an hour in Bracknell and £40 a week in

Waltham Forest, based on an average eight hour day. Irrespective of whether they had attended a course or not, the minders in the sample were aware of this current rate and claimed that they charged accordingly, with just one or two in each area stating that their fees were slightly above or below. Despite these claims, Table 6.1 indicates that almost half of the providers were, in fact, earning less than £1 an hour.

Table 6.1 Hourly rates of pay for childminders in the two study areas

Hourly rate	Bracknell	Waltham Forest
less than £1	5	9
£1	5	5
more than £1	5	1
Total	15	15

In some cases the hourly rate was well below £1. One experienced childminder, who had for years actively campaigned in the local association to improve childminders' conditions of work, was herself earning £35 for a 50 hour week. A colleague charging £30 for a full week's provision was earning the princely sum of 66p an hour! Indeed, the number of hours for which day care was provided seemed to explain, at least partly, the strikingly low hourly rates; especially amongst childminders in Waltham Forest, where nine were working for more than the 40 hours a week on which the pay guidelines were based.

Interestingly, a very similar picture had emerged from our earlier survey of 200 childminders. While generally indicating that they based their fees on locally established rates, over half were calculated to be earning significantly less when account was taken of the numbers of hours worked. Our current findings thus confirm a picture of childminding as a poorly paid occupation, in both absolute and relative terms. This was underlined by one of the Bracknell childminders, who pointed out that the mother whom she charged £1 an hour for childcare also paid her £3 an hour for doing her ironing! By the time of the study's follow-up, almost a year later, only 15 of the 30 day care arrangements were still operating. We shall look at this finding in more detail later; here, it is appropriate to note that in only eight of these cases had the charge for day care been increased, and in half of them, the initiative for doing so had come from the parent! One childminder commented with apparent pride that she had not put her fees up in four years: 'That's not bad is it?' The implicit view that self-denial in this area was a virtue recurred many times in the childminder's references to the financial aspect of day care provision. It could also go some way towards explaining the otherwise surprising finding that the great majority (almost three-quarters) of the minders in the study expressed themselves content with the payment received for their work. Another significant factor here, however, was the extent to which they saw childminding as contributing a vital part of their family income. Thus, statements of satisfaction were almost invariably qualified by explanations that the money was not of great importance.

'It's purely pocket money.'

'I could manage without the money. I mean, I enjoy looking after children... it's just an extra bonus.'

'I spend it on luxuries. I don't need to work... it wouldn't break the bank if I didn't childmind.'

The bulk of complaints about levels of payment came, correspondingly, from those to whom income from childminding was crucial – a situation much more common in the London Borough than in the county area. Thus, one minder who claimed that:

'I rely on it 100 per cent now – it pays for my holidays, children's toys, clothes, sometimes the milk bill...'

described the basic level of charges for childcare as

'ludicrous – (mother) will pay £3.25 an hour for a cleaner and she pays me £1.20 an hour for looking after her child. It doesn't make sense.'

Yet the fact remained that even those childminders who were economically dependent on the work were as likely as not to declare themselves content with what was, by any standards, poor remuneration. This was a perplexing picture which required further explanation, and insight into the factors which influenced the way in which childminders perceived the financial aspect of their work.

Our findings suggested that this was a complex issue in which a number of elements played a part. One of these was located in the private market framework in which childminding arrangements took place, and involved a practical recognition that the fee charged was as much as parents could or would afford. The message conveyed by the pre-registration course that parental circumstances

should be taken into account had seemingly entered the conscious-
ness of many childminders: 'There's no way that (parent) could
afford the chart (*sic*) prices'. One Bracknell minder who had declared
herself 'disgusted' with the level of pay for childminding nonetheless
held the view that:

'I don't think you could ever (get) a reasonable fee for the long hours,
otherwise parents couldn't afford you.'

While most of the comments of this nature focused on the
consumer's perceived ability to pay, there were also hints of more
benevolent considerations influencing childminders' approach to
charging for their services. One of the Bracknell study members,
explaining why she had not raised her fees after a year, said: 'I don't
see the point in ripping them off because it's pointless them going out
to work'. Another childminder in Bracknell, who had only increased
her fee a year later when the mother concerned had insisted,
confessed that: 'I tend to think more of the mother paying than me
earning'.

This implicit concern for the position of those using their services
points to one of the major factors underlying childminders' antipathy
towards the financial aspect of their activity, and consequent
resistance to exhortations to be more 'businesslike' in its conduct.
This factor is connected with the *personal* nature of the relationships
involved in a childminding arrangement; not only between the adults
on each side, but also the configuration comprising childminder,
parents and children. We saw in the preceding chapter how feelings
of personal rapport, that the various adults and children involved
would 'get on' and 'take to one another', were crucially important
considerations in the decision to go ahead with the day care
placement. From the point of view of many childminders, the need
to maintain and develop such relationships ran counter to a concern
with money. Thus, one Waltham Forest childminder maintained
that she was: 'happy with the fee because (mother) is just like a
friend'. Another pointed out that she: 'liked to count my mums as
friends – not your "money-grabbing-on-a-Friday" lark', and a
colleague in the same area commented that she was:

'not really working for money – I want one thing, a good relationship – with
childminder and mother understanding.'

Punctilious adherence to the formal aspects of the agreement did not
combine easily in the childminder's eyes with the pursuit of friendly

relationships. This was nowhere more evident than in the application – or, more accurately the *non-application* – of specific terms of the contract covering matters such as absence through sickness, or holidays and overtime charges. One Waltham Forest minder, whose standard contract stipulated full pay for the first week of a child's absence through illness and half-pay thereafter, felt herself unable to implement such conditions:

'If (child) is sick more than a week – I don't *want* any pay because it's not *fair*. If she is not well, how can they pay money for me?'

A colleague in Bracknell admitted that she would not pursue her contractual entitlement to payment when the child in the study did not attend for some reason.

'Technically, if he doesn't come to me because he's going to his nan's or something, I ought to be paid. But it's something I've never pushed... it's a lovely relationship so it doesn't matter.'

Several minders in both areas commented that they often would not exact their agreed charges for overtime in cases where parents arrived late to collect their children; in the words of one Waltham Forest minder, 'I don't think that is friendly'. The view of a colleague on the same topic implied that the formal terms and conditions of the contract were of trivial importance compared to the maintenance of a harmonious relationship: 'When you are happy with each other you don't go and pick on silly little things!'

The personal nature of the relationships created by a childminding arrangement is closely linked to what lies at its heart, namely, the care of a young child. This, too, represents a potent force counteracting attempts to encourage more businesslike behaviour among childminders, since, as our findings showed, a sense of commitment to childcare and the pursuit of one's own economic advantage did not co-exist comfortably.

A Waltham Forest childminder recounted how she had refused payment when the mother in the study had asked her to provide additional childcare for her son while she visited the doctor: 'I don't want the money... I love him anyway, my boys love him, so, really... I mean...' One of the Bracknell minders explicitly summed up the perceived conflict between childcare and an entrepreneurial approach:

'You have to look at it as a business if you want to be successful. But you *can't* look at it as a business towards the children. You have to be in a way a second mum, their best friend.'

Thus, the affective element at the core of childminding does not easily allow for pecuniary self-interest. The 'good' childminder is one whose prime motivation for undertaking the provision of day care is essentially altruistic, a view which received wide endorsement among the providers in our study.

'If you just want to get money, then go and get an ordinary job outside. You should want to do it because you love children.'

'You're either in it for the money or you're in it for the children'.

It is interesting to note that this same view was expressed within the training context, at least in one of our study areas. In Bracknell, the day care advisers laid stress on 'love of children' as the most salient characteristic of the good childminder, and when interviewed, the experienced provider who gave a presentation at the pre-registration meeting, expressed criticism of the attitudes she sometimes encountered amongst participants.

'They've got it in their minds that they're going to stay at home and earn money. I don't think that is the right attitude. You've got to do it because you love children... the money's a secondary thing.'

When this is considered against the message of the session urging a more business-oriented approach to childminding, it is clear that training, as it currently operates, contains at least two messages which are somewhat difficult to reconcile.

The parents' perspective

Before moving on to the implications of this for the future development of training, it is important to look at how the financial aspect of childminding was viewed by the other party to the private transaction, namely, the parents. Interestingly, our findings pointed to a mirror image of the provider's perspective which we have described above. As noted earlier, parents expressed a similar dislike of the whole process of discussing and exchanging money in the context of childcare. For many of them, however, these negative feelings were bound up with the highly-charged ambivalent emotions experienced when it came to entrusting the care of their child to someone else, especially a stranger.

'I found the money side of it a bit embarrassing... it seems sort of incidental... (child) is so emotionally close to me that I don't like to talk about paying somebody to look after her.'

'It's the fact of *paying* somebody to look after (child)... it doesn't seem as *nice* as having someone you trust look after him. It sort of puts it into perspective that they're doing it for the money and it makes you feel like I'm just sort of dumping him with somebody all day for money...'

The tension between money and the affective core of childcare, which was so evident in the accounts of the childminders in the study, was expressed with equal clarity on the parental side:

'I feel embarrassed about giving the money really... she is obviously so attached to him already – I think of it more as a friend looking after him for me.'

The discomfort with which both sides approached the issue of money may well have contributed to the fact that, contrary to the scenario depicted on the pre-registration courses, very little negotiation as such appeared to have taken place over the financial terms of the agreement. In general, minders explained their terms, referring to local guidelines, and parents accepted them. Where, as in Waltham Forest, these guidelines were also made available to *parents* before entering into discussion with a prospective childminder, this was considered helpful. As one father put it: 'Because it's all laid down by Waltham Forest that does make it easier'.

With regard to the basic fees for day care, the parents in the study, like the childminders, appeared accepting of the amount they were asked to pay. Almost all of the Bracknell parents, and about two-thirds of those in Waltham Forest, said that they considered the basic charge reasonable. As was the case with the minders, however, their views were also related to their personal economic circumstances. Thus, one Bracknell mother who, by the time of the follow-up interview no longer felt financially constrained to go out to work said:

'I'd be prepared to pay (minder) basically anything that she asked... I realise I'm getting very very good value for money.'

Another comfortably-off mother in Waltham Forest expressed similar sentiments, but also pointed out that this did not apply to all parents.

'When you think of what she does for (child) and the time she has her, I mean – the amount of money is really low... and it's low in relation to my salary, but it's probably not in relation to other peoples'. So there's a difficulty there...'

Indeed several of the parents in the study did feel that, given their financial circumstances, day care fees were expensive. This was illustrated by the comments of two young couples in Waltham Forest, each of whom had placed a first baby with their childminder.

'We've had to cut back on things... to make sure we can pay (minder).'

'The wage bracket we're in – we're not working to have luxuries – we're working to pay bills.'

However, just as the childminders frequently adopted the *parents'* perspective in assessing the level of charges, so the users of the services, while lamenting the cost to themselves, were sympathetic to the economic position of the providers. In the words of a single mother in Waltham Forest, who received a contribution from the local authority towards the costs of day care:

'When you can't afford it it seems very hard, but in terms of what they get an hour, it's relatively low.'

Yet although most of the parents in the study considered the childminders' fees reasonable, this did not mean that the financial side of the arrangements was without tension or, in some cases, overt discontent. And, as in the childminders' accounts, the parents' comments indicated that the most common problem areas were the fringe terms of the agreements covering payment for absence and holidays.

It is significant, perhaps, that in as many as a third of the cases in our sample there was a factual difference between the childminder and parent in their respective reports of the terms of their contract. Given the discomfort felt by so many on both sides in addressing such issues, it would not be surprising if the fine grain of the contractual terms had not been discussed in detail when the agreement was reached. In practice, the tendency which we have seen, for many childminders not to pursue their contractual rights on a number of issues, may well have served to avoid potential conflict, since, for a number of parents, these terms were a cause of resentment. The most common source of complaint was the childminders' contractual entitlement to holiday pay. In Bracknell, the general guideline followed was that minders should receive half the normal fee when the child did not attend due to family holidays.

The Waltham Forest contract, however, had gone much further in advancing the interests of providers by stipulating that full fees were payable when both parties took a vacation. The indignation this aroused in many parents is illustrated in the following excerpt from an interview with a Waltham Forest couple, in which the father was himself self-employed.

Father' 'I can't think of any good reason why anybody should have to pay for somebody's holiday... if they are just a casual employer. I mean she is not taking care of (child)... I really don't see why we should give her £80 just before she goes off to Marjorca!'

Mother: 'She's taking up a place – that's what it's about – taking up a vacancy.'

Father: 'But there *is* no vacancy – she is in Majorca! And we have to find another childminder – I don't see how that can be right.'

Mother: 'My God – you are really talking about serious money!'

Although, in a number of cases, both parties noted they sought to take holidays simultaneously, this did not always prove possible. One couple, who felt it was 'unfair' to pay full fees to cover both occasions, had negotiated with their childminder to pay half the amount as a retainer while she was away. However, as the mother pointed out, this still represented an unwelcome financial outlay for the parents: 'That's £20 – but then, she'd find us another child-minder and we'd have to pay her as well!'

The concept of the retainer, paid to childminders for holding places open, was a common one in both areas, particularly in relation to the provision for teachers' children, who did not attend the childminder during school holidays. It will be recalled that a number of the providers in the study expressed a preference for looking after such children, in order to have school holidays free to devote to their own families. This subject was not without problems, however, as illustrated by a case in which a Bracknell teacher requested day care during the summer vacation. In the words of the childminder concerned:

'She said to someone, "If I have to pay my childminder anyway, I might as well pay her the rest and she might as well have her!" '

The indignant childminder consulted the day care adviser on the matter, and was informed that if she refused to take the child, her retainer fee would be forfeited. The numerous terms and conditions which the increasingly sophisticated contractual agreements seek to cover are thus highly complex, and the intricacies and implications relating to the diversity of childminding arrangements have, it seems, yet to be fully recognised. As the disappointed childminder quoted above added:

'Social services have just come up with a new contract which is supposedly foolproof... they're just learning what should be on a contract and what shouldn't.'

In both areas, the childminding contract contained clauses setting down the childminder's entitlement to pay when a child failed to attend through sickness. Although in practice, as we have seen, several minders did not exercise this right, its very existence was, for some parents, a matter causing resentment. This was especially likely when they themselves suffered loss of earnings when they took time off work to look after the children.

'With teaching, it's difficult to take days off. If (child) was extremely poorly I'd stay at home, but I'd have to pay (minder) and I wouldn't get paid for not going in.'

Is childminding work?

The foregoing findings from our study highlight the tension surrounding moves to advance the interests of childminders as *workers*. Any improvement in their conditions of labour leads directly to a negative economic impact on those who use their services. At one level, this tension lies in the framework of personal negotiation which childminding, in its private form, necessitates. Here, in contrast to the publicly-regulated context in which services such as nursery provision operate, every transaction of the agreement is immediately visible in terms of gain or loss to one side or the other. In the nursery situation, matters such as sickness and holiday absence are absorbed by an organisational framework without any direct impact in terms of cost, time and stress on the individuals concerned. In the childminding setting, however, the potential is created for invidious comparison and discontent. This is all the more evident in cases, including some of those in our study, in which the precarious financial circumstances of users and/or providers rendered the business of childminding a potentially fraught area. As a father in the study pointed out:

'If you started to run it more and more like a business then... I think that what will happen is that probably fees will go up, then it becomes something that people like us perhaps couldn't afford.'

At a more complex level, our findings have shown that encouraging a more businesslike approach among childminders challenges the underlying perceptions, held by many providers and users alike, that childminding is not an activity which actually merits occupational benefits. The paradox contained here was illustrated in the responses of the study participants when asked whether they considered that childminding was a 'real job'. About two-thirds of the childminders gave an affirmative answer to the question, although, interestingly, several added that it was the fact of payment which made it so.

'I suppose I do yes... I mean it's something you're being paid for, so it's got to be a job.'

'Yes – the financial side more than looking after the children.'

One or two others expressed the view that the home-based location of childminding detracted from its significance and status in occupational terms.

'It took me a little while to think of it as a job... I think when you work from home – that adds a certain stigma to it... not necessarily the childminding but anything you do at home – I think it's not the same as going out to work – sort of not "real" work.'

Another childminder, echoing the commonly held view among her colleagues that society generally does not perceive childminding as a genuine occupation, attributed this to an equation of childminding with the traditional female domestic role.

'A lot of people think it's money for old rope – getting paid for changing dirty nappies, feeding them – which every woman can do.'

The parents, too, expressed divergent opinions on the issue. While the majority claimed they did see childminding as a job, the fact of payment and, interestingly, the contractual basis, were important contributory factors.

'I suppose it is because they get paid for it.'

'The contracts and everything make it pretty much like a real job.'

It was also interesting to find that some of the *mothers* in the study emphatically supported the notion of childminding as a job, and added that it was a highly underrated one in view of the responsible and demanding nature of the work. A couple of *fathers*, on the other hand, while seemingly endorsing this view, went on to describe childminding as a 'vocation', 'comparable to nursing' – a perception which links more strongly to the motivation of altruistic commitment than to that of occupational self-interest.

As with the childminders themselves, however, a minority of the parents did not consider childminding to be a 'real job' at all, seeing it as, in the words of one mother: 'something they're doing extra to what they'd be doing at home anyway'. Another mother made a revealing reference to an unfortunate incident over the payment to her childminder.

'I had a cheque bounce once – my bank made a mistake with my salary. It was so embarrassing – I sort of explained what had happened. It could have been a real business thing and it would have been even worse!'

It is also important to note the words of one of the fathers in the study whose acknowledgement of the occupational status of childminding was tempered by criticism of the absence of public regulation.

'I see it as a job being done by people with very little job training or professional guidance – it's not a job in the sense that if someone went into a factory they would... be very closely supervised. I get the impression that they are almost left to get on with it.'

It is important to recognise that the ambivalent views regarding the nature of childminding as work, which were articulated by the minders and parents in our study, have for long permeated the sociopolitical fabric of our society at all levels. We can recall our earlier quotation from the member of parliament who, in the 1946 Parliamentary debate, referred approvingly to those who were motivated to offer day care out of good neighbourliness, and contrasted them with 'people that are going into childminding as a business'. That such distinctions still prevail was illustrated by an Assistant Director of Social Services in one of our study areas, who spoke critically of childminders who may be 'doing it primarily as a job'.

At the heart of the dilemma confronting the attempts to professionalise childminding in the ways we have described, lie the dominant ideologies surrounding the activity of childcare, the role of women as carers, and the status and rewards of domestic labour. The care of young children has been, and is, overwhelmingly perceived as the responsibility of women; childcare in its broadest sense is equated with 'mothering' and as such, is regarded as instinctive, natural and unskilled. Finally, such care, as in childminding, takes place in the home – a private domain in which women's work has been traditionally unrecognised, undervalued and unremunerated. It is in the context of such powerful traditional forces that we have to set our examination of the trends in childminder training to promote a more businesslike approach to the work, to assess its achievements to date and future chances of success.

Discussion

The main thrust of training for the business side of childminding urges providers to be more organised and efficient in establishing the boundaries of their work, and the terms and conditions under which it is offered. The analysis of our 30 sample cases suggests that the recommended use of contracts, and the informed awareness of local guidelines to which pre-registration courses drew attention, were regarded by childminders – and parents – as constructive and helpful. However, though our findings revealed few overt problems, they did bring to light underlying conflicts and ambiguities in the perceptions of the main actors involved in the childminding scene, and in the structural framework in which it is played.

The distaste and embarrassment with which many childminders and parents approach the business aspect of the relationship has its root in their perceived need for personal rapport and understanding as the basis for a mutually satisfying arrangement. Thus, the business of childminding cannot be treated in isolation from other features which contribute crucially to its quality. To suggest, as current training strategies appear to do, that the tension inherent in the negotiations between childminder and parent can be diffused by a more explicitly businesslike approach by the provider, is to disregard the emotional context in which the exchange takes place. At worst, such behaviour could serve to *alienate* the prospective consumer, since, as we have seen, many parents expressed deep suspicion of childminders whose motives were seen as primarily economic. As childminding currently operates, a highly sensitive and delicate balance exists, whereby parents are willing to recompense childminders for their services, as long as the latter appear acceptably disinterested in reward.

It is important, therefore, that, in addressing the business aspect of childminding, training courses help childminders to be aware of, and deal with, the ambivalence which so many experience in equating the pursuit of business with the affective component of childcare. But the feelings of *parents* in this context are equally complex and fraught with conflict, and there is clearly a need for more information, guidance and support to be available to them in raising their awareness of the perspectives of both users and providers of day care.

Other shortcomings, however, are less easy to resolve. Training which seeks to equip childminders to treat their activities as a business venture flies in the face of a social reality in which many – providers and users included – do not see childminding as an occupation at all. The structural context in which childminding is conducted acts to reinforce such a perception. The private market setting, in which the terms and conditions of day care are negotiated, produces a situation in which childminding cannot represent a viable source of income. At the same time, charges which are low – even by the standards of home-based workers – place severe strain upon the earnings of a great many parents.

Training, operating as it does within a policy framework which retains childminding firmly within the private domain, cannot hope to resolve the problems stemming from these practical and emotional obstacles to turning childminding into a business. There is a strong case for a more radical change, which would remove responsibility for financial negotiation and transaction from the shoulders of childminders and parents, and place it, like the operation of subsidised schemes, under the auspices of social services departments. During the course of our interviews, the childminders in the study were asked whether they would welcome such a move. As we had found in our earlier survey, the balance of opinion was strongly in favour. The perceived advantages, interestingly, reflected the very objectives which the training courses, in advocating a more business-like approach, had sought to achieve.

'That would be better – you'd know at the end of the week you're going to get your money.'

'Yes – childminding should be recognised as a job... and the benefits of the job should be passed on to childminders – a decent salary, holiday – which most people at work can have.'

'Oh brilliant idea – brilliant! That's the only bit of the job I don't like. For all the years I've done it, that's given me the most headaches.'

In the absence of any such radical change in the context in which childminding is provided, it is hard to see how training – or any other strategy for that matter – can make a major impact on its occupationag status. In the present situation, the counteracting forces, which locate childminding so firmly in the undervalued, underpaid domain of female domestic labour, would seem to prevent any major progress in the direction of 'turning it into a job'.

7. Relationships in childminding

'It isn't a piece of luggage you leave at the station for the day is it? You have to interact.' (Waltham Forest mother)

'I don't think there is a word – it's not a business relationship, it's not a friendship. It's a common interest I think.' (Bracknell mother)

The strong emotional threads running through the whole process of a childminding placement were evident in Chapter 5, in which we looked at how parents and childminders first came together and agreed upon their day care arrangement. Parents' feelings of ambivalence and anxiety about entrusting the care of their child to someone else were matched by the childminders' concern that the two families would be compatible, and that the parents would prove reliable clients. In the view of both parties, the establishment and future success of the arrangement were largely dependent upon a sense of personal rapport among all the individuals concerned; that is to say, the childminder and her own family on the one hand, and the parents and their child(ren) on the other.

All this points to the importance of personal relationships in determining how well childminding arrangements work. It also raises a key question for the present study – namely, how does childminder training address the issue of the relationships involved in childminding, and what impact does it have on how these are conducted? The potential role of training in this area is highlighted by the framework surrounding childminding. As we have noted, this is characterised by *privacy*, with the result that the parties concerned are largely left to map out for themselves their respective roles and relationships. This contrasts with the group care setting in which, notwithstanding recent changes in the direction of empowering parents in their dealings with professionals, the formal institutional structure gives shape to the interaction between service users and providers. In the absence of a formal or institutional structure, questions arise concerning the balance of *power* between childminder and parent; an issue which has received scant attention in previous research. A further significant difference lies in the individualised nature of childminding, which means that any difficulties which arise in the relationships between the adults or children concerned cannot be mitigated, as it can in the nursery setting, by regrouping or rearrangement of personnel. These characteristic features of child-minding indicated some of the key items which would need to be included on a training agenda concerning the subject of the relationships in this type of day care.

The design of the research enabled us to examine in some depth the relationships within our sample arrangements, both at the outset and as they had developed almost a year later. The living reality of these relationships is, of course, a complex configuration involving all the adults and children concerned. For clarity of presentation, however, we break them down into separate areas of analysis, beginning with the relationships between childminders and parents.

Childminder-parent relationships

In the previous chapter, we identified a somewhat uncomfortable coexistence in the minds of both childminders and parents of the formal, especially the financial, aspect of the arrangement, and what they saw as an essential personal component. Our interviews with both groups explored in more depth how these two dimensions were accommodated in their respective views of what the relationship between minder and parent *should* be like. The findings revealed a striking diversity of opinion both among and between providers and users, with varying degrees of emphasis on the importance of a business relationship, personal friendship or a complex combination of both. Echoing the distaste for the notion of childminding as a formal commercial activity described in the previous chapter, about half of the childminders in the sample stressed the importance of friendship between the adults involved. This perspective appeared to derive from their emphasis on the *child* at the centre of the day care arrangement, and the essentially affective, personal nature of their task as carers.

'It's not a product, it's a *child*, so it has got to be friendship really.'

'It's too much of a personal service to be business... because you're looking after someone's child... there has to be trust, the parents have to feel confident in me and we have to be friendly and happy... so the children feel they're coming to a friend.'

But there were aspects of the childminding situation which led providers to a different view. The remaining half of the sample were equally divided between those who saw their relationship with parents as a mixture of two elements: 'You need to have a "friends" and a "business" side to every parent relationship for it to work' and others who believed in maintaining a certain distance from their adult clients. From the views expressed, it seemed that a preference for formality was based on the notion that familiarity breeds possible exploitation. As two childminders, recalling earlier unsatisfactory experiences, pointed out:

'Some parents will work on the friendship angle. They will try and get away with more because you get fond of the children... you can get too friendly and they put upon you.'

'It should be business to keep everything straight, because once it gets too friendly that's when little things start creeping in (for example) about the time – you know: "Oh – she won't mind" sort of thing.'

This sense of unease attaching to the childminder-parent relationship was highlighted by the fact that providers were not alone in such apprehensions. Several parents intimated that they, also, were wary of overstepping invisible boundaries by becoming over-friendly with their childminder.

'What worries me is if you.. become too close then maybe you start to do things she doesn't like and she can't say to you and vice versa. That is why I prefer it to be professional.'

In general, parental views on what the user-provider relationship should be like were almost equally divided between those who saw it primarily as a business association, a friendship, or a combination of both. As with the childminders, the perceived need for personal rapport hinged on the child, who was the reason for the arrangement.

'It's an odd sort of relationship... it's got to be friendly because you're saying, "Here is my child – the one thing I care most about". But at the same time it's still a business arrangement in a way.'

In contrast to the childminders, however, the reasons given by parents who preferred to maintain a formal distance also focused on the child, and seemed to reflect an anxiety that developing a friendship with their childminder could make it difficult for them to express their wishes or concerns regarding what took place in the day care setting. As one Bracknell mother put it:

'I would like to get to know her better but... if there were some difficulties it is easier to deal with it if we are not too close as friends... If I had to say to her the care isn't adequate... it is perhaps easier the slightly more distant.'

Another significant point to be made here is that the closer and more intimate a relationship, the greater the likelihood that personal and deeply-held views can and will be aired. In the childminding situation, this carries an element of risk, since giving expression to differing values and beliefs could threaten the harmony of the arrangement. A mother in Waltham Forest observed that:

'You can get on touchy ground if you are too friendly with someone. (Child) is the priority in all of it – I would hate (minder) and I personally to disagree over something and jeopardise what I think is good for (child).'

The comments made by childminders and parents indicated that both parties experienced a need to retain some *control* over a situation which, as we have noted, is subject to little public regulation or social consensus regarding its nature. On the childminders' side, there was a desire to protect the limits of their work role, and the space and time of their own domestic activities. One study participant, who had earlier looked after a friend's child, recalled how she:

'had to sort of cool off the relationship – she was just here all the time. It just seemed to get out of hand and I don't like that.'

Parents, for their part, had a corresponding need to retain a degree of control over what was happening to their children. In the words of a Bracknell father:

'It is one of those situations where... if things become too familiar they start to become uncontrollable – the element of being in control for me is certainly important. You need to be in charge – in a nice sense!'

The foregoing accounts illustrate how the approach of the adults concerned towards the relationship between childminder and parent was characterised by ambivalence and caution. Each side was under conflicting pressure to seek, and at the same time to avoid, close personal contact. From the information we collected for the study, it would appear that current training initiatives in the field of childminding have done little to address these fundamental contradictions in the minder-parent relationship. In the context of different topics, the pre-registration courses in each area emphasised to prospective childminders the importance of being business-like, of establishing their own work boundaries and, at the same time, of being responsive to parents. Yet the conflict which could emerge in pursuing these various goals was not fully acknowledged through any in-depth consideration of what the minder-parent relationship should be. This highly complex topic clearly requires time and skill to be explored in the necessary depth. However, the packed agenda of the few, short sessions which made up the pre-registration courses did not allow for more than cursory coverage. On the Waltham Forest course, for example, there was no opportunity for the tutors to discuss with participants the leaflets from the Open University Training Pack, that were distributed as course material. The training pack included sections on minder-parent relationships which, among other points, drew a useful distinction between 'friendship' and 'friendliness.'

It is significant to note here that very few of the childminders in the study recalled having covered this topic at all in the pre-registration courses they had attended. Those who did, indicated – revealingly – that they remained as uninformed and perplexed as before.

'I think it did mention it but it wasn't an in-depth discussion. It was one of those discussions where... everybody was putting their point of view but you didn't gain any knowledge from it.'

'We discussed how childminders and parents get on – but I think a lot is left for the individual childminder – everybody's different.'

Given the conflicting forces which childminders and parents experienced in developing their relationships, it was encouraging to find that in the majority of the arrangements (about two-thirds), both parties expressed generally positive views of their relationship. However, this did not mean that the day-to-day interaction between them had been wholly free of problems. In the following pages we shall focus deliberately on areas of difficulty which emerged in the communication between childminders and parents, since it is only by recognising their complexity that training measures to improve childminding can become more effective. Before looking in detail at the day-to-day interaction between childminders and parents, however, it is important to consider the respective roles each party played in determining what actually took place in the day care setting.

The power of decision making

One of the key questions in relation to where power lies in the childminding situation is: who decides what the nature of the children's day care experience will be and how they will be treated? We referred in Chapter 4 to the potentially conflicting training messages conveyed to participants on the pre-registration course, that they should be responsive to what parents wanted for their children and, at the same time, cognisant of their own and their family's needs.

The predominant view held by the childminders in the study was that their personal and domestic regime should set the scene for the minded child's day care experience. As one Bracknell provider commented, '(Child) has to fit in with my life, not myself to his life'. The fact that the childminder's service was provided, literally, on her home ground, represented for many the most powerful justification for this view.

'It's my house and I'm the ruler of the roost. If they don't respect the way I bring them up, they don't stay.'

'I don't believe you should change because a parent thinks you should do this and you're doing that; because you're doing this job in your own home, so you're setting your own boundaries – you're your own boss.'

A further important consideration, to which we alluded in discussing childminders' acceptance of placements, was their concern that provision for minded children should not conflict in any way with their treatment of their own. One Bracknell childminder commented that she would be prepared to compromise with parents over minor differences of approach:

'provided it didn't differ too much from the way I treat my own children, because you can't have two standards.'

In similar vein, a Waltham Forest provider explained that she:

'wouldn't force my views on parents – if they want their baby brought up in a certain way, I would try to respect that. But... you want the atmosphere in your home to be happy, or else that's going to affect your own child isn't it?'

A small group of childminders appeared, however, to endorse the view that parents' wishes concerning provision for their children should be paramount. As one Waltham Forest participant put it, 'I have to do what the parents want because she is their child'. One of her Bracknell colleagues, who had attended the course which we observed, recalled that the issue of whose decision should prevail:

'came up on the course… it made me think about it actually – I think I would have to go by what the parents would like – I wouldn't go against the parents.'

However, subsequent remarks by the same childminder pointed to the importance of examining such attitudes in concrete rather than abstract terms. Referring to a recent incident in which one minded child had bitten another, she expressed her shock at the response of the perpetrator's parents that she should have done the same to him!

'I don't smack my own, so I did it in the way I've done to mine. It never really struck me, you know, because I've always carried on the way *I* do things really. I've never really spoken about it to them.'

Such an example illustrates the importance for those delivering training to focus participants' thinking on their own values and practices in respect of specific issues such as discipline, when considering the implication of adopting an accommodating approach towards reproducing those of someone else. It also highlights the fact that, despite the many detailed initial exchanges described in Chapter 5, numerous matters of substantial importance to one or both sides had not been discussed at all. Much of the information exchanged regarding parents' wishes and expectations focused on practical matters such as feeding and sleeping routines affecting babies, rather than respective beliefs and behaviour relating to the treatment of older children. In many cases involving very young, first-born children, parents felt that particular issues were not yet relevant, or were even uncertain about their own views.

'At four months your knowledge is pretty limited anyway. Things come up on a daily basis.'

Even where older children were involved, however, parents acknowledged that numerous matters were left undiscussed.

'You can't go through everything – you don't *think* of everything. It's a lot to do with taking certain things for granted.'

In the light of all the foregoing points, it was perhaps not surprising to find that, almost without exception, it was the childminders rather than the parents in our sample who had the power of decision over how the children in their care spent their day, and how they were treated. The comments of parents on this topic revealed that they shared the views of the childminders reported above – that operating in their own home entitled them to exercise such control.

'I left it to (minder) because I felt quite strongly it's her domain while he's with her.'

'It was left more or less up to (minder) – I felt it was more her territory than mine.'

While many parents appeared to have accepted this situation with equanimity, a few had clearly found it less comfortable.

'It's very difficult – I don't think I would have been in a position to dictate what I wanted him to do in someone else's house.'

'You feel you're sort of *encroaching* on her if you ask her to do anything like painting or playdough.'

However, a quite different factor had also played a part in empowering childminders to determine the nature of the minded child's experience. This was the sense of confidence and trust which the parents felt that they had gained from their initial contacts and discussions with their childminder, and which enabled them to feel relaxed – in some cases somewhat apologetically – about leaving their child in her hands.

'I just trust her I'm afraid! I wouldn't dream of saying, "Can you make sure you sit down and read a book with her today?" '

'I leave it to (minder). I've got confidence in her and she knows I have confidence in her.'

An awareness and expectation of parental trust was also a significant part of the childminder's perspective. As one Waltham Forest provider pointed out:

'The parents trust you well enough to leave their children with you (so) they've got to sort of think – "Well, she's going to look after them as best she can." '

In one or two cases childminders referred explicitly to parental confidence in them as a source of considerable satisfaction. One Waltham Forest minder commented that the parents involved in the study were 'the best I've ever had.' On being questioned further she explained, 'They have so much confidence in me – really, it makes you feel so much better'.

The power exercised by childminders in determining the content and ethos of the minded children's day care experience was, as we shall see, an important factor in the interaction between the adults concerned. In view of this, it seems important that training should do more to instil in childminders a greater awareness of the power they hold, what contributes to it, and its implications for their relationship with parents. It also needs to be pointed out, however, that, while the childminders' control of the situation was not in itself perceived as problematic by parents, it was in most cases based on a high level of mutual *assumption* regarding shared beliefs and practices, rather than explicitly exchanged knowledge, and acceptance of each others' child-rearing beliefs and behaviour. It is within this context that we need to examine the developing relationships between childminders and parents in terms of their everyday contact and communication. In the next section, we turn our attention to this topic and, in particular, to how any emerging differences of view were dealt with.

Contact and communication

The most obvious opportunity for communication between the adults concerned came when children were delivered to and collected from their childminder. It was interesting to discover the extent of fathers' involvement in this routine; in just over half the cases it was mothers who took sole responsibility, otherwise it was a shared task, except in two cases in which it was the father who had almost exclusive contact with the childminder.

It was clear from participants' accounts that the actual amount of contact between childminders and parents was limited by the practical constraints of their respective timetables. Morning delivery was usually a brief ritual as parents hurried to work and, in many cases, childminders took their own or other minded children to school or playgroup. Collection periods were, in general, less rushed, although the length of time parents spent at the childminders' home was in most instances only five to ten minutes. In terms of mutual satisfaction with this situation, however, the actual amount of contact appeared less important than the feelings of each party about the quality of their communication. In one case for example, in which both expressed themselves very satisfied, the mother rarely even went in to the minder's house, but emphasised that: 'it's not something that bothers me – if I feel there's things to be said, they're said'.

In about half of the sample cases, both childminder and parent appeared quite content with the communication which took place between them regarding the minded child and the progress of the arrangement. In some instances, it seemed clear that conducting relaxed, open exchanges presented no difficulty, as the comments of the two parties in a Bracknell arrangement illustrate.

Childmcnder: 'When they pick him up they always sit and have a little chat. I like to tell them exactly what has gone on during the day... I take photos of the children as well so parents can see what a mess they get in! I do think they should be told literally everything because it is their child. It brings the parents into your home.'

Mother: 'I really stay there as long as I feel I want to talk.'

In very few cases, however, did it appear that the two parties concerned had, as in the following examples, explicitly agreed to air any matters they felt were important. A Waltham Forest childminder explained how she told parents that:

'If you don't like anything – tell me straightforward rather than sit and suffer... whatever comment you want to make, please do.'

Similarly, a Bracknell mother described how she and her childminder:

'both said that if on either part we were concerned about anything then we'll say so rather than – you know – keeping it.'

In the majority of cases, however, as in other unstructured social situations, the amount and nature of the communication between childminders and parents appeared to be determined more by implicit assumptions and subtle indications than by such overt statements as those quoted above. Yet when we recall the ambivalence with which many approached their relationship, it is hardly surprising that communication, too, could be charged with uncertainty, and that, in half of the sample cases, one or both parties had experienced some dissatisfaction with their day-to-day interaction. And since, as we have seen, it was the childminders who were largely in control of the day care experience of the children concerned, it is equally unsurprising that parents were twice as likely as minders to refer to difficulty in obtaining information or asserting their own views.

In a few cases, the individuals concerned sought to explain the communication problem in terms of their own personalities. One mother described herself as too shy and embarrassed to spend time talking to her childminder.

'It's me – I just can't stand there and have a long conversation... I would if I was a more outgoing person.'

Another mother, whose arrangement had ended by the time of the second interview, was unhappy with certain aspects of the subsequent placement. However, she felt unable to discuss this with the childminder concerned.

'I prefer to get away... I'm not really one to talk about things, like that – I'd much prefer to change her.'

Such inhibitions were not exclusive to parents. A Waltham Forest childminder recalled how previous clients had frequently failed to inform her when their child would not attend.

'I was angry, but I didn't say anything, I think it's just a fault of mine that I can't – I don't like confrontation with people.'

It seems clear that individuals who have difficulty in expressing their views will find it particularly hard to do so in the comparatively unstructured framework of a childminding arrangement. It could be argued that there is a useful role for assertiveness training here to help both childminders *and* parents to express their feelings and wishes, and thereby negotiate and review their arrangements more effectively. But it is important to remind ourselves of the private, individualised setting in which childminding takes place, and to look beyond particular personality traits to the structural *context* which also influences whether and how views are expressed. This is especially relevant in respect of the childminder training initiatives with which we are concerned here, since the context in which people meet and interact is amenable to change, through, for example, the insights and behavioural changes which such training can produce.

Pressures of time

One of the most obvious contextual barriers to minder-parent communication was the real or perceived pressure on one or both parties not to linger when the child was collected at the end of the day. Many parents felt that they should not overstay their welcome when the childminder had her own family to attend to. It is important to note that such feelings were just as common among parents who were otherwise highly satisfied with their arrangement and their relationship with the childminder. One such mother commented, however, that:

'I don't always get to know all I want. (Child) is usually the last to go, so I just feel I should get out quickly – you know, because it's the end of her day. It seems like it's not a good time to talk because all her kids are there.'

From the childminders' standpoint, although acknowledging the competing demands of their own families, it appeared that parents were also under pressure not to stay and talk.

'They've got to go home and cook... They're obviously tired as well, being at work all day.'

The implicit messages thus conveyed by each party to the other could lock them into a set of perceptions which created a barrier to effective communication. This was illustrated by one case in which both childminder and parents expressed critical dissatisfaction over their interaction.

Mother:	'I just get in and go – if you see she's busy, you tend not to want to ask.'
Father:	'Yes, you don't want to sort of disturb her.'
Mother:	'I try to say, "You look like you've had a hard day", but I just don't... she always seems so busy, I don't want to intrude.'
Childminder:	'They just come in and pick him up – they never really sit down and have a talk about him.'

A training objective which sought to help childminders become more aware of the impression they are giving to parents, and of parents' reactions to it, could do much to avoid situations of this kind, in which each party sees the other as the obstacle to desired communication.

There were a few examples, however, of how childminders had subtly manipulated the situation in order to facilitate a daily exchange with the minded child's parent. One Waltham Forest provider ensured communication by deliberately not having the child ready at collection time.

'I always let the mother come and sit down and *then* I put the kid's clothes on. If there is any problem I will tell them.'

The catalogue of information which the minder then recited raised some doubts, however, about whether the mother would have been gratified to receive it!

'If (child) has bumped his head, or hasn't eaten, or hasn't slept, or has been naughty or sworn at me, or hit somebody or bitten someone – I give them all these details before they take the kid away!'

In one or two other cases in which delivery or collection periods were not considered conducive to proper discussion, this would take place at other times. As one Bracknell mother said:

'I'd *make* time. If I was rushed in the morning or evening I'd phone her and see how things were.'

However, shared perceptions of what alternative forms of communication were welcome could not be taken for granted. A Bracknell childminder, who had been happy to receive regular lunchtime phone calls from the anxious mother of a first baby, referred to the hostile reaction of some of her colleagues.

'They said – "I wouldn't have that – it's disgusting – checking up on you, making sure you're there – intruding. She should go to work and leave him!"'

This illustration of the variation in response to even the *means* of communication underlines the delicacy and sensitivity of the childminder-parent relationship, and helps explain the caution and uncertainty with which it was approached. It also highlights the major task facing training programmes – to raise childminders' awareness of the importance of communicating with parents, and to equip them with the skills needed to pursue open, direct discussion of matters crucial to the mutually satisfactory conduct of their day care arrangements.

Pressure to conceal conflict

As we have already observed, it was impossible when arranging the placement for the two parties to discuss every aspect of childcare which was of current, or future, importance to them. Consequently many of their respective beliefs and practices became apparent only as the arrangements progressed. In our second interview with childminders and parents, we asked whether any differences had emerged in their approaches to childcare and, if so, how these had been dealt with. Their responses indicated that perhaps the greatest obstacle to open communication between childminder and parent was the pressure to suppress disagreement.

As many as half of the parents in the study acknowledged some difficulty in conveying to their childminder the fact that her day care provision did not wholly meet their wishes or correspond to their own treatment of the child. Some made it clear that they avoided such conflict as a possible threat to the continuation of the arrangement. As one mother put it:

'I suppose it's... you've got a childminder, it seems to be working, you don't want to put a spanner in the works. You decide whether it's worth actually bringing something up.'

The extent to which parents could feel constrained to remain silent, even in the face of extreme concern, was illustrated by the disturbing case of a two-year-old who had visibly been smacked by her childminder.

Mother: 'I didn't really like her being smacked but I never actually came out and said it to (minder) because you feel almost beholden to the person that's looking after your child.'

Father: 'We felt very much in (minder's) hands. We were very concerned that she was going to say, "That's it – I'm not going to have her tomorrow" and we would be dropped in a situation where we've both got to go to work – who do we get to look after the kids? So we felt very much that – crikey, we've got to grin and try and keep her happy!'

In this case the childminder concerned was, by her own admission, flouting the explicit local authority view on physical punishment which had been presented at the pre-registration course. The parents, for their part, clearly felt unable to act in the interests of their own child. This worrying case, although an isolated one in our study, serves to highlight most forcefully the fundamental weakness in a form of day care which is not amenable to public supervision to ensure the welfare of the children for whom it provides.

The most common inhibiting sentiment described by the study respondents reflected the perceived need to avoid what could be construed as complaint or criticism. Numerous examples were cited by parents of the difficulty they experienced in expressing their concern. One mother when travelling on a bus had been alarmed to see her child left outside a shop.

'I'd never do that – all this abducting going on. But I didn't like to say "Don't do it". I just said "Do you say think he'll be alright?'

Another mother described how, after discovering that her son was left to sleep in his buggy by the childminder, she 'gingerly mentioned' that she preferred this not to happen.

'That was the first thing I'd ever suggested to her. I was *trembling* – because I really didn't want her to think I was complaining.'

The most striking example, however, concerned a mother who, while in her childminder's house, heard her small son crying in the toilet. She quoted the childminder's response to her:

'She said, "I'm not having this nonsense – this is just because you're here". And I was staying in the kitchen – very embarrassed, wanting to be with (child). Anyway, I didn't intrude.'

While such inhibited feelings were most commonly expressed by parents, some childminders also indicated that they found it difficult to broach differences of approach to childcare. Thus, one Bracknell minder considered that the mother concerned 'tends to treat the children older than their age – it causes insecurity I think'. She added, however, 'it's her child – it's not my place to tell her the way she should treat him'. Another provider expressed a general view that childminders had to be cautious in probing how children were treated at home.

'You can't go too far because the parent thinks you are trying to interfere in the way they bring up the children. You can't seem to be overpowering or they think you are trying to take over.'

Thus, one or both adults in a childminding arrangement could experience strong pressure not to acknowledge differences of belief and behaviour regarding the care of the children concerned. From the parental standpoint, this derived in part from the perceived territorial prerogative which entitled childminders to exercise control in their own home environment. From the minders' perspective, a determining factor was the parents' personal power in relation to their own children and how they should be brought up. But for both parties, an equally potent force appeared to emanate from the nature of childminding itself, in particular, the extent to which it is seen to resemble parenting and the experience of routine family life. Differences in child-rearing practices at home and in the day care setting will, of course, occur in other forms of provision, and those involved will find it similarly difficult to express their concern. What is specific to childminding, however, is that it brings into close juxtaposition the values and practices of two *family* regimes, so that any overt expression of difference readily becomes, by implication, a criticism of the other's parenting. Unexpressed concerns and disagreements can, however, become the source of simmering discontent, and it is important that training efforts should seek to help childminders – and parents – to communicate as openly and constructively as possible.

The contribution of training

In both study areas, general emphasis was laid in the pre-registration courses on the importance of minder-parent communication and the need to discuss fully matters of respective concern regarding the day care to be provided. Participants were urged to exchange views on issues such as play activities, house rules and methods of discipline and, where differences emerged, to seek a compromise. However, given the limited time available on the courses and the inevitably superficial coverage of such complex topics, it was hardly surprising that only four childminders recalled having discussed them at all. Their comments on the sessions concerned reflected the vagueness of the message which had been received: 'They did say that if you can communicate with parents you can get on a lot better'.

By contrast, the comments of the Waltham Forest childminders who had attended the 10-week college course in that area, suggested that the more in-depth approach of that training initiative may have made more impact. As one participant put it: 'The different things they spoke about they really delved right into'. Another recalled in detail the context of the course and indicated that the different training technique adopted had had some influence on her thinking about minder-parent relationships.

'In several situations we had a role play where sometimes the coordinators were childminders and we were the parents, and you would get to see the parents' point of view. Plus the coordinators would get a chance to feel how it would be to be in the childminder's shoes.'

The same childminder emphasised the need to recognise and acknowledge different values and behaviour rather than keep conflict covert.

'There are certain things that I feel strongly about – but if you do things in a different way, if you sit down and *talk* to parents about it, it makes a better relationship... you can't put over the angle that you know everything.'

It was impossible to assess whether, and to what extent, such views had been directly influenced by the childminder's training experience. However, it is reasonable to assume that any response would be conditioned by a predisposition to accept or reject particular ideas. It is pertinent to note, therefore, that another Waltham Forest childminder who had attended the same course, also recalled the sessions on 'getting on with parents', but felt that the experience had enabled her to be more confident and assertive in pursuing her original beliefs.

'We were really told – don't keep nothing under cover. If you want to say something just come out and say it. If the parent don't like it then she will have to go to another childminder. If she doesn't like your views, your disciplining her children, she should be at home looking after them herself. You know, it really boils down to that!'

Training strategies which seek to address such complex issues as minder-parent relationships and communication thus need to uncover, and respond to, the different and deeply-rooted attitudes which participants bring to childminding. To do so effectively requires considerable skill and time. As we have seen, however, time was a scarce commodity on the pre-registration courses, so that all too often trainers were unable to pursue adequately such revealing comments from course members as: 'It's the parents that are the problem, not the children'.

The power of knowledge and experience

Before leaving the topic of childminder-parent interaction, it is important to examine further some of the views expressed during the interviews with the two groups, since they highlight another significant dimension of their relationship. Basically, this concerns the extent to which variations in child-rearing practice, to which we have referred to above, were accepted by those concerned as 'different' or condemned as 'wrong'.

A typical example of the latter perspective involved a childminder who, having persuaded the child in her care to drink from a cup, was annoyed to find that she was still given a bottle at home.

'I am not one to tell her what to do, but... I felt like giving up! If they were trying to rectify (*sic*) it I would have had some sympathy.'

In several cases, childminders gave subtle – or not so subtle – indications that they saw themselves as possessing greater childcare knowledge and experience than parents, and hence, having a legitimate right to set the minded child's developmental agenda.

'I want to (toilet) train him – we have to talk about how we are going to work it out because there's no point in me training him here and she doesn't take no care at home.'

Embedded in such remarks is the notion of the childminder's superior parenting. At its most explicit, her own childcare skills were contrasted with the parents perceived inadequacy.

'They need educating! I mean – parenting doesn't come naturally to some people so they need guidance. I mean – (child's) mum – she didn't have parents here to guide her so she needed pushing in the right direction sometimes – like with her food. So... just to talk about it set her thinking and a few days later she would change.'

Given that childcare forms the core of childminders' work, it is understandable that they should regard this as an activity at which they excel. All too easily, however, this can lead to invidious comparisons between their own behaviour and achievements, and those of the parents of the children in their care. Several child-minders in the study recounted with undisguised pride how they had succeeded where parents had failed. For example, one provider, whose minded child, not untypically, behaved better with her than at home, quoted the mother concerned: ' "How do you do it?" she'd say – "what have you got that I haven't got?" '. Another claimed to have established feeding and sleeping patterns for a baby who 'never had any routine at home – now she's an angel'. Childminders' sense of their greater experience and knowledge of childcare added to their authoritative approach in determining the nature of the day care provision – especially in the case of first-born babies. One provider explicitly stated that:

'say if you were looking after their third one – then possibly you might have some problems – because they've already had two so they've got their views.'

Such findings as these points to another source of power in the childminder-parent relationship, namely the power of knowledge and experience. It was interesting to find that many parents in the study, especially those with young, first babies, perceived this in a positive light. One such mother referred to her childminder as 'a woman of wisdom – I'm still in L-plates!' Another couple in the same situation were similarly appreciative of their childminder's acknowledged experience.

Father: 'We haven't had a child before so we haven't got the faintest idea!'
Mother: 'I've got very little personal experience so I'm quite happy to be led where she points.'

Clearly, however, the way in which parents responded to the knowledge and experience of their childminder depended greatly on how this was communicated to them. As one Bracknell mother pointed out, she was able to accept and welcome her childminder's intervention because:

'she's very diplomatic – she doesn't make me feel inferior... she doesn't say "Oh, you ought to do this, you ought to do that." '

It was also interesting to discover that, in three of the sample cases, a considerable age difference between childminder and mother had contributed to what resembled a mother-daughter relationship between them. As one father commented to his wife during the interview: 'It's like having your mother isn't it – it's like taking the baby to his nanny'. Another such case, however, revealed the powerful emotional undercurrent flowing through the childminding situation. Here it seemed that the close mother-daughter relationship which appeared to have developed between childminder and parent had lowered the barriers to overt expression of conflicting views on child rearing. During the first interview, for example, the minder commented that the child was:

'grumpy this morning because she went out last night and he didn't get to bed till 10.30. And I said, "Well, if you put him out of his routine he's going to play you up. They need routine don't they?" She'll learn!'

The mother in question was, at one level, highly satisfied with the day care arrangement and cheerfully acknowledged her childminder's authoritarian approach.

'I just feel completely happy – in fact she pulls me up on things. When I'm feeding him she'll say "Pick that bottle up – all that air going into him!" And: "You shouldn't take him out without a cardigan" – just like my mother does! I've been banned from giving him pudding!'

At another level, however, the mother was clearly angered at the childminder's behaviour.

'There are things that she's told me that are right – but it's hard for somebody else to tell you isn't it? When they start telling you, you feel really resentful.'

The comments of the childminder concerned vividly illustrated the ambivalence and uncertainty which she, too, experienced in terms of the boundaries of her relationship with both mother and child.

'Sometimes I think – well, should I say that? Should I mind my own business? But then, I've got to have him in the day – and he's miserable. Surely I've got a right to voice my opinion – or have I? When anything like that comes up... she gives me the impression that I'm "just the child-minder" then. I haven't got to express my opinion on what she does with him.'

We have discussed at some length the notion of the childminder as 'superior' mother which was detected, albeit implicitly, in the views expressed by some providers in our study. It is important to do so, not only because this would seem to represent a potentially explosive element in the already-sensitive relationship between childminder and parent, but also because our investigation of pre-registration training courses revealed ways in which this notion could be unwittingly reinforced.

In the interview with one of the Bracknell course tutors, she described how, in an understandable attempt to avoid an alienating, didactic approach to participants, they would:

'start off by telling them that we haven't asked them to come because we think they need to know about how to bring up children. They've probably all done it – and done it well!'

At the end of the observed course, another tutor commented that, in relation to the subject of child development, the participants had 'all got the knowledge there – they've proved it to us – we haven't really had to lecture them'.

A video entitled *Through the eyes of a child* was presented at the first session and showed a series of everyday events in the life of a mother and toddler. Afterwards comments were invited from participants, which produced a welter of criticism of the mother's behaviour, ranging from lack of suitable conversation to inattention to safety and inadequate discipline. Although the tutor subsequently pointed out that 'we're not here to criticise', it did seem that, in the context of a training exercise required for registration, the participants' response was to seek to demonstrate their own parenting skills (and implied suitability for childminding) by identifying another mother's shortcomings.

A further example of how the Bracknell course subtly reinforced invidious comparison between childminders and mothers came in a presentation by a health visitor, which went far beyond imparting information on health care and first aid. In stressing that it was up to the childminder to decide whether to accept sick children, the health visitor commented:

'a lot of (mothers) will do anything to leave children with you when they really ought to be at home with mum.'

In the context of discussing the complex and sensitive topic of child abuse, and how childminders should deal with it, she remarked that she:

'would think that the majority of people who put their children in your care do it because they've got good jobs... They're actually better at work, they know they can't cope with small children. That is probably the best decision they've made – because if they had the children all day they would probably throttle them!'

It is disturbing in itself that employed parents should be pathologised in this way, as a possible danger to their own children. It is all the more so in the context of childminder training, since it lends support to the underlying critical view of parents held by many childminders and the linked notion that they themselves are 'better' mothers. Such a view militates against the development of minder-parent relationships based on mutual understanding, and the acceptance of alternative beliefs and practices as different rather than inferior. Childminder training needs to raise awareness of participants' own values and behaviour, and of the diverse approaches to child-rearing in a multicultural society. In doing so, trainers have to be particularly alert to the implicit messages and assumptions which may be embedded in the material they present.

The minder-parent-child triangle

So far, we have focused on the relationships between the adults involved in a childminding arrangement. Even so, it has been clear that the minded child is ever present in their interaction, either literally, or as the main subject of their exchanges. Our investigation of how the children concerned fitted into the complex relationships we have been describing showed that this, too, is a highly emotive area, and one which can create tension and conflict for those involved.

The views expressed by the childminders in the study indicated that establishing a close, affectionate relationship with the children in their care was seen as a prerequisite of a successful placement – especially in the interests of the children themselves.

'I think you should be quite close to them so that they feel safe with you.'

'To a certain extent you've got to make up for their parents not being there.'

The references made to the children in their care suggested a high degree of emotional involvement on the part of the care providers.

'I love them and care for them as if they were my own children.'

'Once I have looked after them for a year I have got the feeling that they are *my* children – I looked after them, I changed their nappies, I washed them…'

Their comments also pointed, however, to the delicate balance which they felt had to be maintained in terms of the boundaries of the respective relationships.

'After all – you're a substitute mother for the child, although you're not trying to take mum's place.'

'I can't get *too* attached otherwise I would be taking over the mother role – he would be looking to me for comfort and love where he should be with his mother.'

Meeting the minded child's needs was thus seen to require a close relationship with the caregiver and emotional commitment on her part. At the same time it was essential to preserve some distance, to avoid intruding on the parent-child relationship. This is clearly a difficult equilibrium to achieve, as evidenced by one case in which the childminder had at the start referred to the danger of over-involvement, but, by the end, was about to terminate the arrangement for that very reason.

'We're so much in tune – I treat him as a son rather than actual work.'

In all but five of the study cases, childminders and parents were united in their view that the relationship between caregiver and child was a close one. It was clear too, that for the parents concerned, this was a source of satisfaction and reassurance.

'They have a lovely relationship – there's a lot of respect there between them. (Child) obviously feels safe and secure – he will go to her with almost anything, which is very important. I'd hate to think he was with somebody that he couldn't trust... or go to with any problems or be able to cuddle up to if he'd hurt himself.'

'I just get the feeling that (minder) is very fond of (child)... that she likes having (child) around. That's very comfortable to go to work with.'

But conflicting emotions were expressed by at least a third of the parents, who acknowledged that they often felt torn between concern that their children should feel close to their caregiver and the sense of resentment and jealousy which this could bring. As one mother said:

'That's a bit hard sometimes. You want them to feel close but you *don't* want them to feel close. I want her to be there for (child) but I don't want (child) to only want *her*.'

Another mother summed up the mixed emotions she felt when she left her daughter, apparently contented, in the company of her childminder: 'It's good that she's happy. Why isn't she crying?'.

Clearly, there is an emotional tightrope to be walked by the adults involved in a situation which requires sensitivity and awareness of others' feelings. In some cases this appeared to have been managed very successfully, as in one arrangement in which the mother described her childminder as:

'very clever and thoughtful. You can see she cares for the parents too... she is channelling him to understand that "I am (minder) – your mother is different." '

However, given the emotional satisfaction which, as we have seen, childminders can derive from their relationships with the children in their care, it is obviously difficult to ensure that this does not adversely affect parents. Several childminders in the study described with barely concealed relish that children were more responsive to them than to their parents, or sometimes showed reluctance to go home. One referred to an occasion when she had visited the child's home for his birthday party.

'We sat down and talked – and he wouldn't dress up. I said "Give me everything – I'll do it!" He came straight to me – I dressed him, brushed his hair – I did everything in his house. So – you know – he listens to me wherever he is!'

The emotional turmoil which such situations could create for parents was vividly described by a mother who occasionally had difficulty in extricating her son from his day care setting.

'It hasn't got any easier. Like, some days he doesn't want to come home – if he's sort of engrossed in a particularly fun game and I'm in a rush... he'll sort of scream his head off and kick and punch me as I'm bringing him out. I could wring his bloody neck, you know? Because there's (minder) – she's saying, "Oh, you must go home", and I'm thinking, "Don't bloody talk to him like that – as if he doesn't want to come home with me. He's *mine* – I'm taking him *home*!" '

The pervasiveness and power of these underlying tensions in the triangular relationship involving minder, parent and child are emphasised by the fact that each of the above examples were drawn from cases in which both the adults concerned expressed general satisfaction with the arrangement and with their relationships.

The potential conflict and confusion surrounding the boundaries of these relationships were further exemplified by responses to a question about who 'took charge' of the child when both childminder and parent were present. The replies showed quite different perceptions *among* both groups according to whether they were based on the notion of territorial power or parental rights. Thus, among the childminders the following divergent views were expressed:

'If it was in my house it would be me.'

'I would stand back – I'd feel I was butting in if she was stood there.'

Similar discrepancies emerged in the responses of parents:

'It's her house and it's her domain.'

'I naturally think – he's mine – so I should do whatever, because I feel that when I'm there she's off duty as it were.'

In some cases minders and parents expressed similar perceptions, in others they did not. The variation of view illustrated above, however, reveals the potential for confusion, misunderstanding and unspoken resentment, in the deceptively simple matter of who disciplines, comforts or dresses a child when two adults are present. What actually happened in the cases in our sample appeared to be based mostly on conjecture or assumption regarding each other's views. In only one instance did a respondent mention that this question had been explicitly aired. This was a Waltham Forest father who remarked:

'This was one of the things we discussed – that if she saw (child) doing something she wouldn't wait for me to say something. That's what we're happy with.'

The foregoing findings regarding the interaction between minders, parents and children reinforce the complexity of these relationships, and the need for childminder training to address the issue in greater depth than is possible within its present format. As was the case regarding adult relationships, the pre-registration courses in the two study areas referred in broad terms to the need for childminders to display affection towards minded children, without fully pursuing this in terms of the conflicting pressures and emotions which could be experienced. Thus, in Bracknell, during a session on the emotional aspect of childminding, stress was laid on the necessity for participants, in the words of one trainer:

'to have some feeling for the children – because once the door's closed and you're on your own, only you know what's happening to those children'

– a tacit recognition of the potential vulnerability of children in a day care setting in which public supervision and regulation is inherently difficult.

On the same course, in considering the role of the childminder in relation to the children in her care, reference was made to research indicating that children can cope with several carers as long as the care is consistent. This presents a positive perspective on how day care can make a beneficial contribution to children's wellbeing and counters the pervasive, but unfounded, view of the adverse effects of maternal employment. However, the description of the child-minder's role as 'doing as much as the mother would, but never taking her place' does little to address, in concrete terms, the very real difficulties which we have seen childminders may face in delineating the boundaries of that role. Such abstract prescriptions, while hinting at the potential dilemma, offer little help in resolving it.

Problems in the minder-child relationship

It is also pertinent to point out that no amount of training can, in itself, ensure that affective relationships between childminders and children actually materialise. Here, it is important to return briefly to the five cases in our sample in which the minder-child relationship appeared to have been less than satisfactory. In four of these, the arrangement had terminated by the time of the follow-up, and two childminders refused to be interviewed a second time. From the accounts given by parents, it was clear that the child's experience had been far from happy.

'It was quite a struggle to get her to go in the morning – I mean, she would cry and not want to go in. (Minder) would just sort of take hold of her and shut the door. She didn't sort of comfort her or anything… she's not a very warm person.'

'(Minder) always sounded cross when she spoke to (child).'

'I didn't feel there was any affection there… when (child) sees (minder) now she'll hide – she won't even acknowledge she's there. It makes me feel guilty, it makes me feel angry. It put me off childminders!'

In just one case it was the minder, rather than the parent, who expressed concern and frustration about the quality of her relationship with the child concerned.

'He didn't relate to me in any way. I feel (he) was punishing me because he felt his mum shouldn't be leaving him with someone.'

It was not possible, of course, to disentangle the complex sequence of events and feelings which had produced such unsatisfactory outcomes. One or two points, however, may be of some relevance. First, for four of the five parents concerned, childminding was not the form of day care which they had wanted. In all five cases, one or both of the adult parties to the arrangement indicated that *their* relationship was not good, that they had difficulty in communicating, and that their views on childcare were very different.

The picture which emerged in this small number of cases, therefore, was of a downward spiral of interacting negative experiences, in which every aspect of the arrangement became a target for complaint and criticism. In such situations, the isolation of childminding and its lack of structural support become painfully apparent. One of the fathers in the study expressed just this point when he suggested that, in a group setting, the problems experienced might have been avoided.

'In a nursery it would have been less of a one-to-one relationship, which I think may be good, because if there becomes tension between two individuals, there are people around to relieve that.'

The minders' own children

An exploration of the relationships involved in a childminding situation would be incomplete without some consideration of the part played by the minders' own children since, as we saw in Chapter 5, their response was an important factor in the providers' decision to embark upon, and continue with the work.

In all but five of the sample cases, both childminder and parent indicated that the minded child and the minder's own children got on well together. It is interesting to note that four of these five overlapped with those described above, in which the minder-child relationship was unsatisfactory – thus adding to the picture of a configuration of negative factors.

Many examples were given of what were obviously close, warm relationships among the children concerned, who were often of disparate ages. The minder of a three-year-old girl described how her own school-age son was 'the apple of her eye at the moment' and the child's mother also claimed that her daughter 'absolutely adores both (minder's children) – we have trouble sometimes getting her to come away'. Another minder said that her two sons and the minded child were 'like brothers – they were just one big pile in the middle of the floor!' Here, too, the child's mother confirmed this: 'they treat him like a brother'.

While such examples suggest that the minding arrangement was highly rewarding for all the children concerned, further questioning of the childminders revealed that, in at least a third of the sample cases, their own sons and daughters had got on less well with other minded children or had expressed ambivalent or resentful feelings about their mother's work. One minder quoted her young son as questioning whether:

'we *have* to have other people's children in this house – you're here to look after us – can't their mothers look after them?'

Another, who had just given up childminding at the time of the second interview, referred to her daughter's response to the news:

'Mum, does that mean now we get you to ourselves – we don't have to share you with anyone?'

The reaction of their own children clearly had a powerful influence on how childminders approached their work. One, whose sons had not got on well with a previous placement, had:

'promised them faithfully that I would never look after another child that they didn't like, because I made them be nice to her – I'd never do it again. I put her before them – that's not fair.'

The preference which we noted earlier among some childminders to undertake the care of young babies was linked to the implication which this had for their own children's reactions. As one minder put it:

'I find if the child is young – from a baby – a relationship blooms – as though the child is part of the family. Maybe with older children their personalities can clash a bit.'

Another childminder did not want to accept any child over the age of two because:

'they're developed – babies I can mould them into the way I like things done – I don't want other people's children doing what mine wouldn't do.'

This further dimension to the relationships involved in childminding emphasises their complexity and fragility. As we noted above, training on its own can do little to guarantee that the various individuals who are brought together in this way will experience the rapport which is so important to a satisfactory outcome. Training *can* make a contribution in this area, however, by raising awareness, both of recipients' own values and behaviour which are of significance to the childminding situation, and those of the others involved in this most emotive of day care contexts.

Discussion

As the preceding pages have shown, childminding is a minefield of intricate and sensitive relationships involving the various adults and children brought together by this form of day care. For childminders and parents, the complexity lies partly in the conflicting components of a relationship which requires the formality associated with financial and contractual exchanges, and, at the same time, the personal, intimate rapport deemed essential in caring for a child. The situation is further complicated by the uncertain balance of power between childminders and parents in the conduct of their day care arrangement, with the former's perceived entitlement to control in her home environment set against the rights of the latter to determine what happens to their own children.

The complexity and contradictions endemic in these relationships can, as we have shown, present a major obstacle to clear, open communication between the parties involved. Many issues of childcare and other matters salient to the arrangement, which are of importance to one or both sides, become apparent only as time goes on. When such concerns cannot be expressed, the arrangement can be undermined by covert dissatisfaction and discontent.

Given this potentially fraught situation, it is hardly surprising that in only slightly more than half of our sample did it appear that the arrangements concerned had been wholly problem-free; due either to the calculated or fortuitous combination of like minds, or a sensitive awareness of the need to be conscious of, and responsive to, the views of others. In many of these cases relationships which had begun cautiously, within the defined boundaries of the formal day care arrangement, had blossomed into more extensive social contact and friendship, and the anticipation of lasting links after the placement came to an end. Among the remainder of the sample, however, problems of varying degrees of severity were evident, and in a few cases major conflict had led to clearly unsatisfactory outcomes. The following chapter explores these in greater detail.

The training initiatives which we examined for the study had broadly recognised the contribution of positive relationships to the success of a childminding placement. However, within the practical limitations of a brief pre-registration course, it was clearly impossible to address in sufficient depth, and in the necessary concrete terms, the contradictions and paradoxes inherent in these relationships. There was some evidence from our study that the longer, more focused course provided for more experienced childminders in Waltham Forest had been able to address some of the issues in a more effective and influential way. There is also a need, however, for those responsible for childminder training to be alert to any implicit values and assumptions contained in the training material – in particular those which may subconsciously reinforce a view of the child-minder's childcare skills as exemplary and, by implication, superior to those of the parents using her services.

An important role for training in this area lies in consciousness-raising; in enabling those concerned to become aware of the

respective child-rearing values and behaviour which are of significance to them and to others, and to judge whether and how these can
be compatible. And, as we have noted with regard to other issues in
the childminding situation, there is clearly an unmet need for
parents, as well as childminders, to have access to help and support
in dealing with these difficult issues.

It is also important, however, to be aware of the *limitations* of
training in this context, since many of the problems encountered in
childminding relationships are rooted, not in the individual personalities involved, but in the essentially private, isolated framework
within which childminding operates. This provides no public or
social consensus regarding the nature of these relationships, or the
rules by which they are to be conducted. As a result, those concerned
are left to resolve these issues for themselves, a task made all the
harder by a setting in which relationships are highly personal. This
contrasts with the group care situation in which, for example,
relationships are more clearly structured and where personal tensions can be diffused through the involvement of others. A further
significant difference between childminding and nursery care lies in
the former's individualised, home-based setting, and its consequent
parallels with parenting and family care. The overlap between the
day care and home environments in terms of what is provided for
children, and how they are treated, blurs the role boundaries
between childminders and parents, and, as we have seen, can lead to
invidious comparisons between their respective approaches to child-
rearing.

The relationships created by childminding are thus, in many
ways, a unique combination of the formal and the personal. The
minders and parents in our study whose experiences in this area had
been the most positive were those who appeared aware of this
paradox and had, not always easily, found a mutually acceptable way
of dealing with it. Even so, the precise nature of the minder-parent
relationship remained elusive, as the following description by a
Bracknell mother strikingly illustrates.

'I couldn't describe us as friends … it was a very, very personalised business
relationship. Friends are people that you have over to dinner, and you go on
holiday with and you go to their house and it's all… it's not business. And
professional acquaintances are people that you don't have any social contact
with, and you just see them at work – and that's fine. And then there's
childminders.'

8. Aspects of quality in childcare

'(Quality care) is the sort of thing you're aware of when it's absent. Basically things like good food, hygiene, security measures, common sense and a certain amount of warmth and love... and I think it's the role of the childminder to stimulate the child.' Waltham Forest father.

In this chapter we turn to what was actually provided for the children whose day care arrangements we were investigating. The nature of their experience was obviously of central importance to the study since improving standards of provision is, as we have seen, a major, broad goal of childminder training. Also, the quality of care for young children looked after outside the family has become the focus of increasing interest and concern among researchers and policy makers, as well as those providing and using such services. It is all the more disturbing, therefore, that so little research has been undertaken in this country on the subject of day care in general, and childminding in particular, and that our knowledge of the nature and effects of such provision remains limited.

The few major studies of childminding to date have tended to modify, rather than contradict, the alarming picture painted by the Jacksons in their albeit somewhat impressionistic accounts in the 1970s (B. Jackson, 1973; S. Jackson, 1971; Jackson and Jackson, 1979). Subsequent investigations in London by Mayall and Petrie (1977; 1983) and in Oxford by Bryant and others (1980) concluded that a substantial minority of children, far from thriving in the homelike atmosphere with a motherly caregiver for which child-minding has been officially advocated, appeared passive, subdued and retarded in language skills. It is important to point out, however, that their assessments of the quality of care were based on child behaviour and minder-child interaction observed during the course of a research interview, an approach which is clearly open to methodological criticism. It is also somewhat paradoxical that Mayall and Petrie, while challenging the perception of childminder as substitute mother, nonetheless based their negative assessments on comparisons between children's interaction with their caregivers and with their mothers.

A more positive picture of childminding emerged from a study in Staffordshire, which concluded, on the basis of more structured observations, that the overall standard of care was of a satisfactory quality, with the majority of minded children being 'provided with stimulating and loving adult attention and... a good range of toys and equipment' (Davie, 1986). Like the other researchers referred to, Davie also noted that children behaved differently at home and with their childminders, but pointed out that this applied to other preschool settings also, and should not be considered surprising or necessarily disturbing.

When we look at recent research elsewhere, we find that investigations in the field of day care have become increasingly complex. With the accumulation of a large body of evidence to refute the widespread popular belief that day care, as such, is harmful to children, it has become clear that simplistic comparisons between children receiving care at home or elsewhere are uninformative (Belsky and others, 1982; Belsky and Steinberg, 1978; Clarke-Stewart and Fein, 1983; Phillips, 1978). Similarly, inconsistent and inconclusive findings concerning the relative effects of different *types* of day care, notably nursery care compared with childminding, have led researchers to focus instead on variations *within* forms of provision (Clarke-Stewart, 1987). The search for global effects has thus been superseded by attempts to disentangle the complexity of day care settings and identify the specific features which are associated with particular outcomes. As Belsky (1985) has put it, the issue has become one of seeking the conditions that define quality or 'growth-facilitating care'.

The approach of recent quantitative studies, especially in the United States and Canada, has been to examine the relationships between various *structural* factors in the day care environment (for example, group size, adult-child ratios and caregiver training), contextual *processes* (such as caregiver behaviour, activities and adult-child interaction); and a range of child-based indicators of socio-emotional and/or cognitive-linguistic development (Philips, 1989). Although the findings of such studies are not altogether consistent, they have identified a range of variables as important components of high quality care, in terms of particular child development outcomes.

Among the investigations which have included childminding settings, a Chicago-based study suggested that features associated with positive child-based outcomes included:

'a neat, clean orderly physical setting organised into activity areas and oriented to the child's activity;

a caregiver whose interactions with the child were responsive, accepting and informative, and

(peers) who were older and more mature and so could set a good example for the child.' (Clarke-Stewart, 1987)

In Canada, the Victoria Day Care study found that the quality of family day care (childminding) homes was much more variable than that of centres, and that in the former, high ratings on a home environment rating scale were positively associated with children's performance on standardised measures of language development (Goelman and Pence, 1987). However, the authors also point to the importance of the interaction between the day care setting and children's family life and background; their research indicated that those from 'high resource' families (with two parents having high levels of education, income and occupation) were more likely to be found in better quality day care settings.

The present study

Such quantitative studies as those referred to above add considerably to our understanding of the relationships between aspects of day care and children's development, and highlight the complex, multi-dimensional nature of the concept of quality provision. For a study such as ours, however, with its in-depth focus on the nature and impact of childminder training, such an approach was, for several reasons, neither practicable nor wholly appropriate.

The major question which we sought to address with regard to the content of the care provided for minded children, concerned the messages which the training efforts in our two study areas sought to convey on this topic. Of course, given the limited resources and specific objectives of the courses on which the research focused, it would have been unrealistic to look for marked, or even measurable, effects on the broad and complex area of childcare practice. Rather, we were interested to see how the material presented related to the views and practices of the childminders at whom it was targeted and of the parents whose children were placed in the minders' care. In this context, it would have been inappropriate to administer any standard assessments of child development, since it could not be assumed that such outcomes reflected the day care objectives of the various parties involved.

It is important to consider also the beliefs and assumptions which shape any research investigation. Notwithstanding its basis in the methodology of scientific enquiry, research can never be entirely objective, since underlying values and orientations will inevitably influence not only how it is conducted, but also the type of questions which are asked. Thus, the determining framework for most of the research described above has been the theoretical domain of child development. With this perspective, the search for quality in day care focuses on features of provision which contribute to specific aspects of child development, especially those which are predictive of subsequent performance in the school system. The research – and practice – implications of such an approach are exemplified in the exhortation of Honig (1988) that:

'quality programmes must be based on child development theories and... enlightening research that emphasise both important programmatic goals and teaching/interacting *processes*, to decrease risks of mental health problems, social delinquency and educational failure later on.'

It is not denying the validity of such a stance to point to the existence of alternative perspectives which might guide the search for quality in day care. The late Jack Tizard (1976), for example, challenged the assumption, which has permeated the research community, that the expansion of pre-school education needs to be justified in terms of long-term benefits to school performance. He argued instead that the immediate well-being and happiness of children and families was a valid indicator of 'success', and sufficient argument for service provision.

It is particularly important to be aware of alternative value bases when investigating a form of provision – childminding – in which, by virtue of its privacy and diversity, consensus regarding what constitutes good quality care cannot be taken for granted. If quality were to be defined solely in terms of what promotes children's development, it would seem to follow that those best placed to prescribe optimal provision would be professionals with specialised knowledge of this field. Such a perspective, however, would deny the role of service users and providers in defining quality, a position which would be ethically questionable, and practically counterproductive to a study seeking to understand how childminding actually operates and the contribution of childminder training.

Perspectives on quality

Our examination of the care offered by the childminders in our study thus took into account what they themselves considered important aspects of provision, and, linked to this, how they perceived their role as carers. Similarly, it was considered essential to discover what parents wanted their children to experience while in the care of their childminders, and how satisfied they were that their wishes had been met. It was within this framework that the objectives and impact of childminder training were examined, in particular in terms of the relationship between these various perspectives on what constituted good quality care.

It was also considered important to present a *holistic* picture of the minded children's day care experience, rather than the decontextualised segments of behaviour and interaction which are the conventional subject of quantitative analyses. The experience of childminding is, for most of the children concerned, one that involves spending a considerable number of hours in the day care setting. The reality of that experience is represented by the synthesis of many features and we felt it was important, in describing and evaluating the provision, to try to retain some sense of its overall texture. There was also empirical justification for this approach, since the following typical interview extracts indicate that what the users and providers of childminding perceived as the ingredients of good quality care reflected the multi-faceted fabric of daily life. Thus, for example, a Waltham Forest mother, when asked what she considered to be the most important elements in her child's day care experience, replied:

'There's always the stimulation and that... but to know that when (child) is not well and he's with (minder) that he'll be perfectly happy to be there – he won't be screaming for mummy or daddy all day. The meals, and general good care – not left in wet nappies and things like that – someone who will care for your child as well as you possibly could yourself, I think, as a basic – and then something else on top of that!'

The indivisibility of the *relationships* involved in childminding and the actual *provision* made for minded children, which is contained in the above quotation, was similarly illustrated in the following responses of a Bracknell couple.

Mother: 'Genuinely *caring* about the children – you wouldn't want them to learn something in a *formal* way'.

Father: 'All we would want them to do is spend the day in a happy, safe environment... feel satisfied that our children are being looked after as closely as we would like to look after them ourselves – the equivalent really of taking them round to granny for the day.'

The replies of the childminders to the question concerning what constituted good quality day care, revealed the extent to which they too perceived such provision as approximating, as far as possible, the experience children would have received at home.

'Good quality care is where there's lots of stimulation inside the home and outside; where the childminder would take the children out... nurseries, playgroups, parks, shopping – anything where a mother would take her own children – everyday settings.'

One of the most detailed descriptions came from a Waltham Forest childminder whose account, reproduced in full below, highlights not only the multiple dimensions of day care, but also the issue concerning the balance between the childminder's domestic and childcare roles. In addition, the account draws attention to the less than straightforward question of how far the day care setting can and should replicate the child's home environment.

'Well, a comfortable home, obviously with all the right things, you know, kitchen, bathroom, toilet, etc. A good diet, which means three meals a day provided if necessary. Willing to give them lots of loving tender care, and I think that should come at the top of the list. I think they should come first; whatever you do in your home your job is to look after the children, and they should be top. I think they should have plenty of fresh air and go out every day. I think the home should be clean and tidy. I don't think you should live in an environment, you know, sort of germ free constantly... a fanatic about housework, because I don't think that works with children. I mean, I know – I've been a bit like this myself. But I mean it just doesn't happen. You do work when you can and keep it clean within reason. I think you should have safety precautions, gates on the stairs, save falling down. You should make sure cleaning materials are all out of harm's way and that children can't get to anything like poison. And you constantly keep an eye on them to make sure they're not getting into mischief where they're going to harm themselves, even just with furniture. You've got to have eyes everywhere. Safe toys to play with, because I think while they've got toys to play with they won't be touching other things, or hopefully they won't. I suppose I should say you look after them like you look after your own really, but some people don't look after their children as well as I would like them to, so perhaps that would be wrong to say that; you should look after your minded children as well as you look after your own children.'

All of the above quotations raise important and complex questions regarding the childminder's role in caring for children and, as we shall see, the ways in which training addresses the various aspects of the provision which they offer.

Despite deliberately adopting a holistic view of the care provided for minded children, we have, for ease of presentation, organised the following discussion of our findings into a series of key 'themes', namely:

- extending the child's horizons;
- fostering social relations with other children;
- forming an affectionate relationship with the child;
- providing a safe, secure environment.

In reality, of course, these themes overlap and interrelate, but they represent the broad areas of provision which were most frequently and specifically referred to by childminders and parents alike, as key elements in good quality care. They were also addressed as such, in some way or other, by the pre-registration training courses in the two study areas.

Having drawn attention to the necessity of being aware of the values underpinning a particular research approach, we should also state explicitly that, from our own knowledge and beliefs, we too would endorse the above areas as essential ingredients of good quality care. In addition, however, a further aspect of childcare which we would regard as important, and one which also featured in the Waltham Forest training curriculum, is founded on an *awareness of the inequalities* in our society – especially those based on race and gender. Child rearing is not impervious to such divisions and we feel it is vital that childminders do not reinforce them, either in their assumptions or their practices.

Observations in the childminding setting

Before turning to the study's findings concerning the care provided by the childminders, it is important to refer to another source of data for this part of the enquiry. In the 15 arrangements still continuing at the time of the follow-up (approximately 10 months after the first interview), the childminders were asked if the researcher could spend some time in their home 'to get an idea of what it's like for the minded children while they're with you, and also of what childminding is like for you'. All but three of those approached agreed to this; two were unwilling to participate and a third felt unable to owing to illness.

Two observation sessions of approximately one hour each were carried out in all of the 12 cooperating cases. Continuous narrative notes were made for five-minute periods at a time – the aim being to preserve as much detail as possible about the child's and minder's activities and interactions. This approach was modelled on the naturalistic observations carried out by Jean Piaget (Piaget, 1977) in his descriptions of children's intellectual development. A tape-recorder was also left running, with the childminder's express consent. During each five minute observation bout, we specifically noted any occurrence of examples of the four themes identified above. Unlike the contemporary emphasis in ethologically-influenced studies, where inference is *removed* and behaviour is observed for the purpose of measurement and quantification, our aim was to conserve detail and meaning, so that inference could be made explicit.

In the following account, findings from the observation sessions will be interwoven with the interview material in order to give as rich and detailed a picture as possible of what the day care experience of children in our sample was actually like. In discussing each of the four themes in turn, we shall also examine the ways in which they were addressed by the training programmes in the two study areas.

Extending the children's horizons

By employing this heading to describe the particular ways in which childminders open out the world to their minded children, we have deliberately avoided focusing on specific, narrowly defined aspects of behaviour. For both childminders and parents in the sample, what was seen as important here was the provision of a wide variety of activities and play opportunities which would stimulate the children's interest, learning and enjoyment.

In the follow-up interviews, childminders were asked to give an account of the most recent day the child in question had spent in their care, plus any other activities undertaken regularly, and to explain what determined their pattern of provision. From the parents, information was obtained on what activities and experiences they wanted for the child, and how satisfied they were that these were being provided.

The often very detailed descriptions given by the childminders revealed both the variety of experience which the day could contain, as well as the way in which its structure and timetable were influenced by the minder's commitment to her own and other minded children. The following account by a Bracknell provider was a typical example.

'She comes here and she goes straight in the buggy and we have to go to school. So we drop the boys off for 9.00 a.m. and she comes in school with me and we say goodbye to my sons – she thinks that's good fun. Then down to the Community Centre, which is near the school, we have Mother and Toddler. Because it's so early we help get all the things out, otherwise I'd have to come all the way home here and then all the way back again, so we stay there. She loves it, she loves it there. She goes and plays and we read books and a couple of times she comes and sees what I'm doing but apart from that she just goes and plays. She has a drink and a cake and she sits with all the children and then we usually leave there about 11:00 a.m. We come home, by this time (other minded child) is dropped off as well. He goes and has a sleep and (minded child) and I get lunch ready. Then we sit and have lunch and (other minded child) wakes up, then we have a play with him. Then in the afternoon we might read or she gets all the toys out, does drawing. Usually its reading, she likes reading, so we sit and read books. Because with (other minded child) around we can – he just crawls all around and (minded child) and I can just do what we want. Then about half past two, if she wants to walk – it depends what the weather's like – sometimes we walk to school, which takes us about half an hour, if she's in the buggy it takes me five minutes! We usually go up the shop and get the boys some sweets and she has some sweets, that's the only time that I allow her to have sweets. We go down and wait for the boys and we come back home here about twenty five to four, and by the time I've got her coat off and given her a drink and put her on the potty, her mum's here. So its all quite hectic and backwards and forwards!'

Parental satisfaction

Overall, about three quarters of the parents expressed a high level of satisfaction with what their minders were providing. In these cases, the accounts of the two parties offered some insight into how their respective wishes and practices coincided. Thus one Bracknell minder who, like many others, emphasised the importance of taking children out as much as possible, described the range of external activities she offered.

'If he wasn't going to the playgroup which he went to twice a week, we'd go out in the morning, maybe to the park to feed the ducks, or we'd go on the bus into town or on the train to Reading – just for the experience of going on a train or bus because his parents drive everywhere.'

The parents in question confirmed their pleasure that their son's experience was being enlarged in this way.

'She's introduced him to new experiences – he'd never been on a bus before. She did a lot with him – she took him swimming, took him out regularly for visits to friends.'

Another Bracknell minder, caring for a child whose first language was not English, explained how she would:

'usually sit down with him in the morning because there's nursery rhymes on TV and a special programme... with counting which helps him with his English. I'm a great believer in learning toys, for example, magnetic letters and numbers – you can put them on the fridge or radiator and you've got an instant game.'

The mother concerned, who had wanted somebody who would give her son a lot of adult attention, was:

'very, very pleased with her... I do believe he has learned a lot from (minder). They read books, sing nursery rhymes, they dance, they play games, they improvise with the toys – what more could I be asking?'

Each of our observation sessions in the childminders' homes provided examples of activities and adult-child interaction which, in our view, contributed positively to extending the children's experience. In the following two extracts, we document the ways in which both minder and parent identified such activity as important, and then present a short selection from the recorded narrative to illustrate how this was observed in practice. (Fictional names have been given to the children involved.)

Case 1

Sophie, aged 16 months, was one of three children cared for by her childminder. Her parents' view of good quality care included the wish that Sophie be 'stimulated with toys and constant contact'. The childminder, for her part, felt that children should be provided with creative activities such as 'painting, drawing... building things, playing with shapes so they get to know their shapes and colours', and be talked to.

The observation took place over two afternoon sessions of an hour each. The minder, Sophie and another minded child, Paul, were present throughout. The following verbatim extract followed a sequence of activity in which Sophie knocked over a tower of bricks, built by the minder, who then helped her construct another.

Minder: Put that one on (the brick Sophie is holding).
Sophie: That.
Minder: Put that one on.
Sophie: (Stacks brick) Look!
Minder: That's it! Clever girl!
Paul: Now make it do this (builds a tower)
Minder: (inaudible) The blue. (Sophie knocks tower over, Paul laughs) You knocked it over! Put that one on. Oops! Steady – no, not yet. (Paul laughs). Yellow one first.
Sophie: Yellow.
Minder: Yellow, that's right.
Sophie: Yellow.
Minder: Then the red one. Put the red one on. Red. Then the white one. Yes. (Sophie vocalises) That's it! Clever girl! Then the blue one.
Sophie: Blue.
Minder: Blue. Then the yellow one.
Sophie: Yellow.
Minder: Then the red.
Sophie: Red.
Minder: Red. (Sophie knocks tower over, Paul laughs loudly).

The focus here is on a simple sequence of actions – building a tower of bricks, and the identification of different colours. The language, too, is very simple, referring to the here and now. This type of talk is typical of other pre-school settings and indicates, perhaps, how the pre-school 'curriculum' has worked its way into the informal atmosphere of the childminder's home.

Case 2

In this example, the target child Fay (18 months) is one of two minded children; the other Joe, is just over two. Fay's parents specified that her day care experience should include stimulating play and conversation, and that she should be taken on outings regularly. Her childminder also attached importance to 'taking children out in the fresh air' and believed that they should be 'learning things every day'.

The observation took place on a hot summer day. During the morning session, the childminder and two children were moving between the kitchen, conservatory and garden. At the start of the following extract, Fay was eating a mid-morning snack, and the minder went into the kitchen to prepare sandwiches to take for a picnic lunch in the nearby forest.

Minder: 'Let me make your sandwiches, then you can help me water the plants outside... We'll go and feed the ducks today.'

She finishes the sandwiches then fills a spray can with water. She takes it to the patio, where a large number of plants hang on the fence, and asks Fay if she has finished her snack. The childminder then rests the can on the ground and turns away briefly. Fay tips the can up and walks off. The minder then turns back and calls to Fay to come and see how the can works. Fay returns and is joined by Joe. The minder shows both of them how to turn the spray on. She gives it to Joe to try and he sprays Fay. They all laugh.

In this brief sequence, the childminder points out the functional aspect of the watering can, just one of the many everyday objects in the children's environment. She also shows that manufactured toys are not the only objects from which children can learn and find enjoyment.

Parental dissatisfaction

Although, as indicated above, the great majority of parents appeared satisfied with the activities minders were providing for their children, it is important to look also at those who did not. In just three cases, parents were clearly unhappy that their children had not been offered the experiences they had wanted for them.

One arrangement had been terminated for other reasons by the time of the follow-up, and the childminder refused a second interview. The parents, however, were ready to express their disappointment at the lack of stimulating activities for their daughter.

'She was there for about nine months – didn't come home with one single drawing. She'd be in front of the telly when I went to pick her up – she learned the theme tune to *Neighbours*!'

The mother added that the childminder had refused her request to take the child to a drop-in centre, commenting, according to the parents, that it was 'just one big pandemonium'.

Similar unease was voiced by another mother regarding how her daughter spent the day.

'I'm not sure that (childminder) chatted to her, played with her as much as I would have done if I'd been with her all day. (Child) got into the habit of watching quite a lot of TV in the afternoons.'

None of these cases were in our observation sample so there was no opportunity to obtain direct insight into what the minded child's experience was like. However, during the second interview, one of the minders concerned indicated a limited perception of the carer's role in encouraging children's learning, remarking that those as young as the child in question (15 months) required little adult input: 'She was only little then – there's not a lot you could do with her'. This minder was not the only one in the sample whose comments raised doubts regarding the knowledge of child development which, as noted in Chapter 4, trainers implicitly attributed to course participants by virtue of their status as mothers. One respondent recalled that the trainers:

'Showed us a lot of toys – books, jigsaw puzzles – but not for very young children. Personally, I can't see... I mean, they're too *young* to be learning. Even he (indicating three-year-old child) won't sit down and read a book, or let you read a book – he wants to take it away from you, then he slings it!'

Although we cannot offer a complete picture of what took place in each case, or a causal explanation for negative findings, there are one or two points which should be noted. It is perhaps significant, for example, that all three sets of parents had been under considerable economic pressure to make a hasty placement, that in all cases little information had been sought or offered in respect of childcare practice by parents or minder, and that communication between the adults remained limited. On the childminders' side, too, there were indications of pressures unconducive to good practice. In one case, the parents commented that the minder, a single mother, was too tired to involve herself sufficiently with their son as 'she's got too many children to look after'. Another minder, also a lone parent, lived in high rise accommodation which, as the parents noted, was an inhibiting factor in taking the children out as they would have liked.

'She's hampered by being in a tower block – to take (child) out is a lot of hassle she could do without – the waiting for the lift.'

Another source of stress mentioned by parents in two cases was the problems that the childminders were experiencing with their own, older children. It seemed, therefore, that both the users and providers of childminding were likely to exhibit the 'low resource' characteristics which other researchers (for example, Goelman and Pence, 1987) have found to be linked to poor quality care. It is important to be aware of these social, economic and personal factors which can influence the way childminders approach their work, since they clearly have implications for the potential for introducing change through the medium of training.

The contribution of training

It was clear from the accounts given by most childminders that the play activities of the children in their care largely reflected the children's own choice. Interestingly, when asked for their views on what activities were *good* for children, they invariably replied in terms of what children *liked* to do. This then determined what they actually did, and in many cases, the minder herself was relatively uninvolved.

'All the children come straight in and into the playroom. They just go and figure out what they want to do. They all tend to find what they want for themselves – they never come and say they're bored. I more or less let them follow their own leads.'

'It seemed as if it was a release to do what (they) wanted – come (here) and run riot, in the sense that there was a toy room, and they could go on the bikes and scoot up and down – races, acting silly and thoroughly enjoying each other's company. I mean, I never needed to do anything on a regular basis – it was basically self-play.'

An important issue arises here in respect of the way in which children's play is addressed by childminder training. In both study areas, one whole session of the pre-registration course was devoted to the topic of play, and one of the messages conveyed was that it should be essentially child-centred and unstructured by the adult whose role, by implication, should be passive. In Waltham Forest, the subject was introduced by showing a video, *Infants at Work*, which demonstrated the role of natural objects, as opposed to manufactured toys, in children's play. The role of the adult, however, was portrayed as largely non-interventionist, the implication being that self-initiated play is necessary for the full flowering of children's cognitive and social abilities.

In Bracknell, too, during a group discussion on young children's communication, a question from a participant on the value of one-to-one adult-child interaction was met with the response that, while necessary, it was important to 'let all the imagination come from them, because (otherwise) you're not helping them to develop or draw things out of themselves'. The implication in both cases is that the process of development is one that is located solely within the child and that the adult should refrain from exerting influence. Such an approach has, however, been seriously challenged by research findings which support a more pro-active stance on the part of adult carers.

This, however, raises a particularly important and problematic issue for childminder training. Although all the sample members who had attended courses clearly recalled the sessions on play, few claimed that they had learned very much, or that their thinking and practice had been influenced in any way. It was clear too that, for them, the salient factor in this situation was their own experience as mothers. As one course participant put it:

'A woman came and talked about toys – we all thought that was boring. You *know* the kind of toys to give a child – we all have children.'

What emerged very strongly here was the extent to which the childminder's role in providing play and activities for minded children was equated with their behaviour as mothers in relation to their own children. In the majority opinion, the fact that they, as parents, had *naturally* provided the play experiences discussed on the course, rendered training on the subject unnecessary and irrelevant.

'I'd always done it with my own – it's just something natural that you do.'

However, a quite different view was expressed by one or two respondents, which is important in emphasising the diversity of values and behaviour attaching to the role of caregiver. This perspective was illustrated by a Waltham Forest childminder who, while also drawing a parallel between the roles of childminder and mother, rejected the training messages on play as being at odds with her own maternal behaviour.

'Most people probably play with their kids – but the way they're teaching us is like organised activities. It's not just like you're a mother... you get up and work around your kids... it's sort of like they're at a nursery and these are the activities they do during the day. But – I didn't do all that with *my* kids, and it might put you off – because I don't think it works out like that really. I mean – you're at home because you're doing other things as well. You're minding because you're at home, not because you want to take kids in to be like a nursery teacher.'

The contrasting views presented above underline the extent to which even the low-key, relatively passive adult role in children's play which was presented on the courses elicited very different responses among the heterogeneous group of participants. It must remain an open question whether advocating more interventionist behaviour on the part of childminders would, in its implicit contrast with maternal behaviour, be more favourably received by those who feel that, as mothers, they have little to learn concerning children's play. What does seem clear, however, is the need for training to address the underlying issue of how far the childminder's role should be, in the broadest sense, explicitly educative, or – as so widely seen by its practitioners – one of recreating the ethos of the home environment.

The use of other facilities

One very practical way in which childminders can contribute to extending their charges' horizons, is by taking them to organised group activities for pre-school children. We have already referred in Chapter 4 to the children's centre in Bracknell, which offered structured weekly play sessions for minded children accompanied by their caregivers. In Waltham Forest there were several drop-in centres, run partially by childminders themselves, but with the involvement of the childminding coordinators, as well as a number of toy libraries and Mother and Toddler groups. The pre-registration courses in each area explicitly encouraged childminders to make use of these facilities, both for their own mutual support and for the play opportunities they offered to minded children.

Nine of the total 15 Bracknell childminders made regular use of the centre, and like those quoted below, cited its benefits to children as the reason for going.

'They have a wider variety of things to play with.'

'There's so much for them to do – and learn to play with other children.'

Four of the remaining Bracknell providers took their minded children instead to a playgroup or toddler group. Only two were uninvolved with external facilities; significantly perhaps, the reasons given indicate how minded children's experience is influenced by the domestic and family commitments of their carers. One explained that it was inconvenient to visit the centre on the day allocated since she had to do weekend shopping; another, that fitting a trip to the centre around delivery and collecting her own children from school entailed, 'too much dashing around just for a chat and to allow the children to play'.

In contrast to the widespread use in Bracknell, just four of the 15 Waltham Forest childminders attended the borough's drop-ins. Here too, the perceived gain to children was given as the main reason for going.

'The children have got more space to play – there is a lot of equipment and a toy lending system. They can do bigger things like painting. At Christmas we have them making cards.'

In addition, however, seven Waltham Forest minders used other facilities, especially the borough's toys libraries, which also offered play sessions, and one worked as a playgroup helper expressly to enlarge the experience of her minded children.

'My main purpose of involvement with the playgroup is so the children I mind can have plenty of activities which I cannot provide in my house – like water play, slides, pastry, doughmaking.'

It is important to note, however, that the remaining four Waltham Forest providers expressed reluctance to become involved with the facilities provided for their use. Two claimed that personal shyness had inhibited them: 'It's just the thought of walking in and not knowing what to do, where to go'. The other two were critical of what they saw as the tendency of participating minders to use the facility as a source of social contact for themselves, to the neglect of the children in their care.

'I have been to toy libraries and things where... I seem to be the only one playing with the children. Everyone else is just sitting there having a cup of coffee and a cigarette. Well, I think it's your *job*.'

Interestingly, the mother of her minded child, a social worker, thoroughly approved of this viewpoint.

'As soon as she said, "I don't get involved with that" I thought, "This is the one for me!"'

Such mixed views were also encountered in our earlier investigation of childminding support services, not only on the part of the minders themselves, but also among the social services workers involved (Ferri and Birchall, 1987). The differences of opinion would seem to reflect potentially conflicting objectives in providing such facilities. One explicit purpose is to offer peer group support and relief from the stress and isolation of home-based work. The need which many providers feel for such provision was eloquently described by one Bracknell childminder.

'When you are in your home, although you are washing up or whatever, you have always got one eye on (them), you are always alert, always ready for something – because children are an accident waiting to happen. Whereas when you are at a toddler group, you can actually let down your guard a little bit, because there are so many people there. So it is a place to unwind really, and literally not worry too much about them.'

The other, often only implicit, goal of such provision is to improve childminders' childcare practice by encouraging their involvement in play activities, and many professional workers express concern that such aims are not achieved (for example, Ferri and Birchall, op. cit.). It seems important that this multiplicity of purpose is recognised by those responsible for such services, since decisions regarding about which should receive priority have implications for the way in which the facilities are organised and resourced.

Fostering social relations with other children

We now turn to the second of the four themes relating to the quality of day care for the minded children in our sample. The opportunity for their children to meet and mix with others was another important aspect of the day care experience desired by all but two of the parents in the study.

Before looking in detail at what kind of peer contacts the children concerned actually enjoyed, it is important to present an overall view of the total number of children involved in the 30 day care arrangements. Table 8.1 shows the number of *other* minded children being cared for at the start of the placement, divided according to whether they were of pre-school or school age.

Table 8.1 Number of minded children in addition to target child

Number	Pre-school only	School age only	Both ages	Total
0				1
1	8			8
2	8	1	2	11
3	2		5	7
4		1	1	2
5				0
6			1	1
Total cases	18	2	9	30

The figures show that, in a third of the cases, the minder was caring for three or more other pre-school children in addition to the target child. (It is important to point out that, because of part-time attendance, cases involving three additional children did not necessarily imply that the provider was exceeding the regulation limit of three under fives in addition to her own.)

As well as other minded children, however, the childminders' own family were also present for all or part of the day care session. Table 8.2 gives a picture of the *total* number of children with whom a child might come into contact in the minding setting. When the minders'

Table 8.2 Total number of children in addition to target child

Number	Pre-school only	School age only	Both ages	Total
2	2	1	2	5
3	1		6	7
4			9	9
5		2	2	4
6			1	1
7			2	2
8			1	1
9				0
10			1	1
Total cases	3	3	24	30

own children are added to the scene, it becomes evident that minded children are not only likely to interact with a considerable number of others, but also to experience a much wider age range of contacts than they would in their own homes or in other pre-school settings.

Parental satisfaction

Almost all of the parents expressed satisfaction with the socialising opportunities available to their children in their day care environment, and several commented that the number and age range involved was particularly welcome. One mother was pleased that the placement offered her only daughter the chance to mix with the minder's own four children plus three other minded children: 'She's got all the advantages of being an only child *and* being one of a massive family!' In another case, in which the minded child was the youngest member of his own family, the mother felt that:

'What he gains from being with (minder) is mixing with other children his own age or *younger* – he's more tolerant of what other children need. It's good training for the fact that you do have to share.'

However, there were also one or two dissatisfactions expressed. Another mother of an only child was disappointed that:

'unfortunately she was just with one small baby – I think it helps if they're with children their own age.'

What needs to be pointed out here is that, in contrast to group care, the presence of other children in the childminding setting is largely the result of fortuitous circumstances. Even if parents are able to take account of this situation when making their placement, there is no guarantee that it will remain the same. The highly fluid nature of childminding arrangements was evidenced by the fact that, in 10 of the 15 placements which were continuing at the time of the follow-up, all or some of the other minded children present at the outset had left and been replaced by others. In one case, this was the chief reason for parental dissatisfaction with this aspect of the arrangement.

'I think (child) was happier with (minder) when there were those two other kids she looked after. (Now he hasn't) anything to stretch his mind like, no older kids to play with.'

The most important aspect of peer interaction was, in the view of both parents and childminders, the opportunity it presented for children to learn to behave sociably with others. Nearly all the parents felt that their children had benefited in this way from their day care experience. One mother, for example, described how, prior to the placement, her son:

'was clingy – going to a childminder helps them develop relations with other people besides their parents – playing with other children they learn relationship skills and how to behave.'

Another mother explained that the opportunity for mixing:

'was my primary thought when I placed her anywhere – being with other kids and learning to be a bit sociable. And I think she's got that.'

Several parents also pointed out that their childminder was offering their children more in the way of social experiences than they themselves could have done. Thus, one couple with an only daughter expressed their satisfaction that:

Mother: '(Minder) took her out more than I would have – she was having the company of other children every day.'
Father: 'I think it's given her a broader exposure to life earlier than if she'd just remained within the family unit.'

A mother who worked irregular hours and whose childminder had readily complied with her specific request that she provide evening meals for her small son, commented that:

'the nicest thing for me is that he sits down to dinner every evening – (minder) has quite a few with her own two and the kids she has after school... so there is quite a crowd of them all sitting down together. They natter and it's lovely, it's a big part of socialising for (child) which I can't ever give him.'

As far as the childminders were concerned, their widespread use of drop-in centres and other pre-school facilities, referred to in the previous section, was also explicitly linked to their view that minded children needed the social contacts which this offered. A Waltham Forest minder who took her charges to two different groups commented that:

'I think it's important to meet other children than just those that are in the house, so they learn to mix and share.'

In our observations of the childminding arrangements in operation, we were concerned to look at the role which childminders played in actively *encouraging* social interaction among the children in their care.

Case 3

In the first example we have chosen to illustrate a childminder's positive efforts in this direction, the target child, Sally (21 months) is sitting on the living room floor with her childminder and another minded child (Justin, aged four-and-a-half). A selection of toys including a toy tea set; is spread out around them. The childminder asks Sally to make a pretend cup of tea for her.

Minder: Can you make me a cup of tea?
Sally: Yes.
Minder: Make me a cup of tea?
Sally: Yes.
Minder: Cheers.
Sally: That (a) cup of tea. (Gives it to minder.)
Minder: Cup of tea?
Sally: Yes.
Minder: Oh, that's nice. Can Justin have a cup of tea?
Sally: Yes.
Justin: I don't drink tea though.
Minder: You don't drink tea?
Justin: Yeah.
Minder: What do you want then?
Justin: Tea.
Minder: You want tea? Can he have a cup of tea?
Sally: (Grunts)
Minder: Give Justin one then.
Sally: Huh. Got one. (Sally gives Justin a cup).
Minder: Is that Justin's?
Justin: (Makes loud sucking noise, pretending to drink tea). Ooh, that's lovely!
Sally: (Vocalises).
Minder: All gone.
Sally: There's another cup.

By means of her intervention, a request that Sally make a cup of tea first for herself and then for Justin, the childminder has brought the two children together in joint play. As this example shows, opportunities for children to interact with each other need not mean the exclusion of the caregiver and may even be facilitated by the adult's involvement.

It was also important to look at how the childminder's practice could make a positive contribution to fostering mutual respect and cooperative social behaviour between children. The following short extract is one of several examples of such practice which was recorded during the observations.

Case 4

It is mid-afternoon and Lee (18 months) is sitting on the living room floor next to his minder, on a cloth spread with toys. Also present are two older minded girls (aged four and seven) who have just come in from school. They are recent placements and Lee is gradually becoming accustomed to them. Their presence means that he has to learn to share the toys, as the following extract demonstrates.

The younger girl (Annie) picks up a toy bus.

Lee: My bus! My bus!
Minder: No, it's not your bus, is it? It's (minder's) not your toys, they're (minder's) toys and you share them. Yeah?
Lee: My bus!
Minder: Annie's playing with it.

The minder makes it quite clear that the use of the toys is open to all and not exclusive to Lee. She is the one who owns the toys and makes them available to the children.

Parental dissatisfaction

One of the few cases in which parents were unhappy about their children's opportunities for socialisation involved a childminder who did not make use of any of the group facilities and who had no other minded children in her care. The parents, having no relations or friends with young children, had noticed that their only daughter 'doesn't relate well to children her own age' and were thus concerned that:

'she definitely doesn't have (social contacts) in the five days a week she's at (minders)... it would have been nice if things like mother and toddler groups had been made use of... I think that is why a day nursery would have been better... get her used to interacting with kids her own age.'

The childminder concerned commented that the time and location of the drop-in facilities did not fit easily with her obligations to take her own children to school. This case again illustrates how particular outcomes are influenced by structural factors in the lives of both users and providers, which are hardly amenable to change through the impact of childminder training.

The interviews with parents also revealed one or two cases in which the minder's actual practice with the children in her care did not seem conducive to fostering cooperative social relationships. One mother described how her son was (untypically by comparison with the rest of the sample) not allowed to take his own toys to the minder's house 'in case there's arguments over who wants what'. Such an approach by the childminder would seem to represent an *avoidance* of the opportunity to teach children to share and cooperate.

As we noted in the previous chapter, a potentially sensitive area in the childminding situation is the relationship between minded children and the caregiver's own sons and daughters. One mother described how her minder's little girl had shown considerable aggression towards her own – 'kicking and shoving her' – and felt that this had not been dealt with effectively, adding that the minder's child was 'really quite upset that there were other children in the house'. However, our observation data also provided an intriguing example of how the childminder's differential treatment of children could prove detrimental to her *own* offspring.

Case 5

The minded child Karen (two-and-a-half years) is having lunch seated at the table with the minder's own son, Ian (aged five) who is off school with an upset stomach. The minder has just reprimanded Ian for dropping part of his roll on the floor. Shortly after, Ian tells his mother that he has finished eating it.

Ian: Mum, I've ate my thing.
Minder: Have you?
Ian: Yeah.. I've ate all of it.
Minder: Good boy.
Karen: No he didn't!
Minder: I bet, yes, I can imagine, Karen, don't worry!
Ian: I did! (Eat all his roll.)
Karen: No! (Inaudible) in your hand.
Ian: I did!
Minder: Let's have a look. I'll come and check, shall I? Hmmm?
Ian: Mmmm, yeah.
Minder: Right.
Ian: I got black stains on me hand now. Tch! (Laughs)
Minder: What else is new?
Ian: I've got black -

Minder: You haven't eaten all of it! Well that's all he's gonna have anyway, Karen, so... I'm sorry, with his bad tummy, 'cos he can't have anything else till dinnertime now.

Ian asks for more food; the minder explains to him that he should not eat any more because of his upset stomach. She leaves the room and Ian takes one of Karen's crisps.

Karen: (To Ian) No! Don't, don't, Ian! (Then to minder) He took one of my crisps.
Minder: (To Karen) Pardon? He pinched one of your crisps?
Karen: Mmmm. (Yes)
Minder: (To Ian) Don't pinch Karen's things, please. She'll always tell me, won't you, Karen? It's naughty, anyway.

This excerpt illustrates some of the rivalries that can exist between minded children and the minder's own children. Karen is described by the minder as being very willing to tell Ian off. Ian, who is five-years-old, does not take kindly to being reprimanded by a two-and-a-half year-old. In addition to this, the minder appears more willing to tell Ian off than to do the same to Karen. This may fuel Ian's apparent 'difficult' behaviour (according to his mother) with minded children. It would seem that the minder's encouragement to the minded child to collude in her criticism of her own son could exacerbate an emotionally fraught situation.

The contribution of training

Both the above examples of problematic relationships involving minded children and those of their caregivers highlight the conflicts and contradictions inherent in the claim made by so many minders that they 'treat the minded children as if they were my own'. There is a role for training here to help childminders explore the beliefs and assumptions which underline such statements. The complex and sensitive area of children's relationships was given little recognition on the courses which we observed, beyond a general exhortation to would-be providers to consider the implications of the work for their own families. More attention needs to be paid to this important issue, in order to raise the childminder's awareness of the impact of the day care situation on the relationships between the different children involved, and of the part played by her own attitudes and behaviour.

Forming an affectionate relationship with the child

The third aspect of quality provision explored in our study involved the relationship between childminders and the children in their care. Warmth and affection from one or more caring adults is essential to the well-being and sense of security of every child, and is the emotional base from which they are able to explore and learn from their environment. We saw in the previous chapter how the pre-registration courses in each area referred to the importance of closeness in the minder-child relationship, and how both child-minders and parents endorsed this view. Indeed, almost all of the adults in the study specifically mentioned *emotional* care, in the form of affection between minder and child, as a prerequisite of good quality provision. Their views were typified by a Bracknell child-minder who referred to the need for day care providers to 'supply the love... (make) the child feel it's wanted', and the parent in the same arrangement who had considered it essential to find 'somebody we felt (child) would be loved by'.

Parental satisfaction

We also saw in Chapter 7 that, despite the mixed emotions which many parents experienced regarding their child's relationship with the minder, the great majority were happy in their estimation that it was in fact warm and affectionate. In this section, therefore, we shall show how our observation data provided further, more direct, evidence of this emotional closeness and the warmth which minders displayed towards the children in their care.

Case 6

The target minded child, Luke (18 months) the minder, another minded child, Tim (three years) (and the observer) leave the minder's home and make their way to the toy library, which the minder visits regularly. The venue is the school hall of the nearby junior and infant school. Inside the hall is full of toys and large play equipment, including a trampoline, mattresses and climbing frames.

About 15 to 20 children of varying ages and racial backgrounds, with their carers, are present. The minder notes the presence of at least one other childminder. As soon as she lets Tim and Luke out of the double buggy, Tim runs off to play. Luke hovers near the minder, watching the other children with great interest. He then joins Tim and two other children who are sitting in a large toy train.

Luke frequently returns to where his minder is standing and raises his arms. She lifts him up and gives him a cuddle. He then goes back to the train.

In this excerpt, we see how Luke uses the minder as a secure base from which to explore the comparatively unfamiliar environment of the school hall. The presence of a large number of other children can be initially daunting to an 18-month-old child, without the reassuring presence of a familiar adult. The fact that Luke turns to the minder for cuddles and that she responds to his requests, is a sign of the attachment between them, an attachment that not only provides emotional security for Luke but also enables him to feel confident enough to interact with relatively unfamiliar children.

In the next observation extract, we see how the affectionate relationship between childminder and child extended also to minder's husband's treatment of the boy, 21-month-old Wayne.

Case 7
The minder's husband, Keith, is about to leave the house.

Minder: (To Wayne): 'Say 'bye, Keith.'
Keith caresses Wayne, says goodbye to him, then talks briefly to minder before leaving.
Minder: (To Wayne) 'Want a cuddle? Let's have a cuddle.' (Takes him to the sofa. Wayne is tired since he did not sleep much earlier in the morning.)
Keith comes back into the house to fetch car keys, speaks to the minder who is attending to Wayne. Wayne slides off the sofa.
Minder: 'You don't want a cuddle? Mmmm? You're tired. Aren't you?'
Wayne: 'Mmmm.' (Assent).
Wayne hovers around the minder, she arranges his clothing, picks him up and takes him over to the window to watch Keith leave in the car.

Finally, one of many examples from our observation data indicate how affection was demonstrated in, and was a necessary condition for, lighthearted physical play between minder and child.

Case 8
The minder and minded child, Rachel aged two, are sitting together on the sofa. The minder begins to tickle Rachel, who laughs.

Rachel: Why are you doing it?
Minder: Nothing, it wasn't me!

Rachel: It was you.
Minder: It wasn't!
Rachel: Yes. (With emphasis)
Minder: It wasn't. (Laughs)
Rachel: It was you, (Minder).
Minder: No. (Laughs)
Rachel: It's you, (minder).
Minder: It's me, (minder) is it?
Rachel: It was you.
Minder: I think it was a... fly. (Rachel laughs) Did you see that fly? Came in there and it went... (tickles Rachel).
Rachel: Do it again.
Minder: It flew off out in the kitchen. (Tickles Rachel, who laughs loudly.)
Rachel: Do it again! (Minder tickles Rachel, she shrieks with laughter.) Do it again!

The minder and child are clearly enjoying themselves and get on well together.

Parental dissatisfaction

None of the observations we conducted produced any contra-indications of minder behaviour in this area – for example, of any overt *lack* of affection towards the minded child. However, it is important to recall the five cases referred to in Chapter 7, in which the minder and/or parent reported during the interview that the minder-child relationship was not satisfactory. Although involving a minority of cases, it was disturbingly clear from the interview accounts that the children concerned were unhappy in their day care environment and that the childminder's treatment of them was, at the very least, a contributory factor.

In the most worrying example, the childminder referred to the minded child's frequent crying, which she considered was 'put on', and to which she responded by:

'just playing with the other minded children – when she didn't want to finish her crying I just left her to sulk... I find the more fuss you made of (her) when she was crying, the worse she got.'

What was significant in such cases was the tendency for the childminder to attribute what she perceived as difficult or problem-atic behaviour in the child to shortcomings in the parents' treatment. Thus, another minder who reported that her minded child was often distressed added that:

'it's obvious that because she's the only one she's really sort of spoiled – it wasn't just like crying – it was literally screaming and yelling – she could disrupt the other kids.'

From such comments, it would seem that the cause of child behaviour which clearly makes the childminder's task more difficult and stressful, was located firmly in the home situation for which the minder has no responsibility. This is no doubt less discomforting than to confront the possibility that it is the day care situation which lies at the heart of the problem. It is significant to note that parents, for their part, could collude in seeking alternative explanations for their child's emotional state. One father, for example, acknowledged that his son did not seem happy with the childminder and that 'sometimes he says he doesn't want to go, but I think that's natural'. It might be hypothesised that, given the mixed emotions which many parents experienced about placing their children in day care, they would be under considerable psychological pressure not to associate symptoms of unhappiness with the fact of being minded.

Only one of the five parents who reported that their child was unhappy with the childminder concerned had ended the arrangement for this reason. The accounts of the others indicated that an unsatisfactory situation had been tolerated in the light of the obstacles to confronting problems in the day care situation which we have identified earlier. One of these was the pressure which considerations of employment and income could exert on parents to maintain their day care arrangement, and not jeopardise the family's economic position. Another, perhaps linked to the first, was the feeling of many parents that they were powerless to intervene in, or influence, what took place in the childminder's domain.

The contribution of training

Some of the factors which we have suggested are in operation here clearly lie beyond the potential sphere of influence of childminder training courses. No amount of training can guarantee the development of affection between caregiver and child which is such a vital ingredient in good quality care. In the courses we observed, the tutors referred to the importance of the minder-child relationship, but also acknowledged that positive feelings and personal liking may not always materialise. From the point of view of the caregiver, it is clearly helpful that this very real possibility is recognised and accepted. In the interests of the children concerned, however, training courses could perhaps do more to enable childminders to confront such unfortunate situations, and, in particular, to engage the cooperation of parents in addressing and, if possible, resolving the problem.

Providing a safe, secure environment

A further aspect of good quality childcare which we need to consider concerns the physical environment in which it takes place, how childminders' practice contributed to this, and how the subject was addressed by training initiatives.

Obtaining a full and adequate assessment of the myriad components of good physical care – safety measures, health care, hygiene, nutrition – would be a lengthy and complex exercise, requiring much more time in the minding environment than we were able to spend. It is important to note, therefore, that all but two of the parents in the sample were confident that their children were well looked after in terms of safety and physical care.

One of the exceptions was a mother who expressed alarm that her three-year-old daughter had been allowed to play outside on a grass verge near a main road: 'I don't allow that – that's totally unacceptable to me'. This mother, while acknowledging that 'in some ways I'm overprotective', was clearly upset by the situation and, as we have found to be a recurrent theme in this study, found it discomforting to air her concern to the childminder.

'I felt she might feel I was criticising... but perhaps there's no other way to take it, because if she was in sole charge of my child, then I *am* criticising.'

There is no way of knowing whether easier communication between minder and parent would have resolved this issue in a mutually satisfactory way. As many users and providers noted, the success of childminding arrangements is, in the last analysis, based on trust and confidence.

In the one other case in which parents expressed disquiet about the physical care of their child, it was clear that they felt their trust had been betrayed. This involved a young couple whose baby had been placed with a childminder living in a high rise block of flats. The father arrived unexpectedly early one day to collect the child and discovered:

Father: 'She had been left with another minder – but she hadn't told her kids who it was. So... I was going up and down – my blood was heating up. Eventually I found her – she was on a chair, lying on one side, sleeping, no one looking after her. I picked her up and walked out.'

Mother: 'That's always the biggest fear I think when you have a childminder, I haven't felt that since she's been at nursery.'

Father: 'I mean – if there was an emergency ... I understood it sort of worked that way with childminders – they help each other out. But she needed to go shopping and (child) was left with somebody she never liked. It isn't what I pay my money to (minder) for!'

This one, as far as we were aware, isolated case in our study provides an illustration of the potential shortcomings of a day care service which is not readily accessible to public scrutiny. Disturbing as the above story is, however, it is also important to note the part played by the childminder's own circumstances in influencing the way she provided care. In this case, her accommodation made it less than easy to combine constant childcare with the routine demands of domestic life.

The contribution of training

Such factors need to be borne in mind when assessing the potential contribution of training to changing behaviour and practice. For, while training may increase minders' knowledge and awareness of good quality care, it can do little to create the conditions in which the provision of such care is facilitated.

The safety of the childminder's home setting is, of course, the subject of inspection as part of the registration process. The pre-registration courses in each area, however, placed emphasis upon its *continuing* importance, as one tutor put it: 'safety isn't something we do once: it's ongoing'.

Participants on the Waltham Forest course were asked to think of any objects or situation which could pose a safety threat to children. This evoked wide-ranging responses, from electrical plugs, alcohol and medicine to small objects of all kinds, poisonous plants and peanuts. Attention was focused on the potential hazards of fires, windows, balconies and stairs. In addition to distributing a leaflet on safety precautions, the coordinators informed participants that equipment such as stairgates, fireguards and a limited supply of car seats, was available to childminders from the social services department. A questionnaire on First Aid was given to course members as a homework task and discussed at the subsequent session. Rather more extensive coverage of First Aid and emergency treatment was included on the Bracknell course, in which the session was presented by a health visitor.

All the study members who had attended courses said that they had particularly valued this part of the curriculum. In common with childminders in other studies, however, this was the single topic on which further training was almost universally desired (Bryant and others, 1980; Ferri and Birchall, 1987). The anxiety remaining after the brief coverage of the pre-registration courses was described by one of the Bracknell childminders.

'I mean, within 10 minutes, you can't get nothing, can you? And I think it's a good thing to know First Aid – I know – I've had accidents with my own children and I've just panicked. Panic *does* set in, you just don't know what to do. I mean, serious things *can* happen – First Aid is something childminders should know more about.'

Issues of equality

In the final section reviewing the quality of day care provided by the childminders in our sample, we focus on the issue of equality and how this was addressed by training courses, particularly in respect to racial background and gender.

Race

As far as the parents in the study were concerned, just one Black mother had deliberately chosen a childminder from a minority ethnic background, in order to help her son develop a positive image of his own racial identity. A further half dozen parents, however, volunteered the view that they did not want their children to be exposed to racist views or behaviour in the day care environment. None expressed any concern over this aspect of their childminding arrangement; but what was perhaps most revealing was that only one of the parents involved had actually *discussed* the subject with their childminder, or had any knowledge of her views on the issue. More typical was the approach of the Bracknell mother who admitted:

'I *should* (discuss it) because it very much does matter – I suppose I just take it on the basis of the comments she makes generally, and I've not heard anything to alarm me.'

It would appear then that racism, like other emotive subjects, is an area in which the constraints on minder-parent communication which we discussed in Chapter 7 are likely to mean that arrangements proceed on the basis of assumption, rather than the explicit exchange of views.

The contribution of training

As noted earlier, the topic of racism featured in the curriculum of the pre-registration course in Waltham Forest, reflecting the authority's policy (incorporated in a council resolution read out to course participants) of promoting good relations between the many different cultural groups in the community and equality of opportunity for all. The course tutors expressed the local authority's expectation that childminders would conduct their work in a non-racist, non-sexist manner.

The session continued with the showing of a video, *The Eye of the Storm*, on children and racial prejudice. The group discussion which followed produced insightful comments from some participants on the speed with which young children internalise the notion of superiority, and the effect which this could have on their learning and behaviour. The tutors used these points to emphasise how important it was for childminders to combat such notions in their work with young children, and asked for suggestions as to how this might be effected. It was clearly impossible, however, to explore this challenging question in any depth, especially in terms of how minders could, in practice, reconcile any conflict in the different cultural values which might be brought together in any day care situation.

It was also evident that remarks by participants which were indicative of an underlying racist perspective went unchallenged by the coordinators, at least within the group setting. (As noted earlier, coordinators reported that they would pursue such issues during home visits to the individuals concerned and, if it was felt necessary, would recommend that registration be refused.) The topic of racism is clearly a sensitive and difficult issue for any training strategy to address, and it seems unrealistic to expect that, within the limits of one brief group session, tutors can create an ethos which enables participants to express their beliefs openly and then question them.

It was no less difficult for us, in our role as researchers, to gain real insight into childminders' views and behaviour in this area, during the course of a wide-ranging interview. Their responses to questions about racial awareness among young children, and their own role as

carers in this context, did not always allow straightforward interpretation, or contribute to a clear picture of beliefs and practices.

Four of the five Waltham Forest minders who had attended the
pre-registration course recalled that the topic had been covered,
although two commented that it had only been 'touched on'. As with
our investigation of minder-parent relationships, it seemed that the
longer, college-based course, and a special multicultural course
which one childminder had attended, had provided the opportunity
to address the subject in greater depth. However, the impact on
participants appeared to have varied considerably.

A Black childminder who had attended the college course felt that
the:

'very basic outline of racism and equality... was good... for people who were
not aware of these things – it brought them awareness.'

She added, however, that as a Black woman who had experienced
discrimination, she was well aware of what racism involved and that
the course had not influenced her own thinking. The comments of
two of her White colleagues suggested that they had found the course
more informative.

'(It covered) play and activities with children from other cultures, and we
did a thing on racism and how you felt about other people, like what would
you do if you got a person who phoned up and asked you what colour you
were.'

'Doing this course has helped me to understand many different backgrounds some of the children come from. If I did have a child that came here
with a different culture, I would understand it I think – I would have the
knowledge to fall back on.'

However, other White minders who had attended the same course
took different views. One was critical of what she had perceived as a
message of positive discrimination:

'They keep drumming it in – he's brown so he should get more attention.
The child should be treated as a *child* – not because he's brown or he's white.
I don't think it's right. You should look after a child as a loving person.'

Finally, one minder in the sample, who was currently caring for at
least one Black child, had clearly misunderstood Waltham Forest's
policy on anti-racist childcare.

'We were told we should be fairly open-minded because there are a lot of
different races and we will be expected to... But on the other hand they said

that (minders) shouldn't take on Black children if they thought they didn't want to... Express their wish to (coordinator) in the first place and say, "Please don't send me Black children." But I've not heard of anyone ever expressing that.'

The difficulty which White childminders may experience in dealing with this issue was highlighted by one Waltham Forest provider who had attended the pre-registration course, and whose target minded child was Black. When shown by the interviewer the population census categories of racial background and asked if she would apply any of them to the child in question, she answered, 'not really – I just treat him as my own – White, really'. The child's mother was conscious of the childminder's difficulties and herself commented that 'I'm sure she sees (child) as White!' She also recounted how, early on in the day care arrangement, the minder's young son had asked his mother, in the presence of the minded child and his mother: 'Mum – is (child) a little Paki?' The mother then described how:

'(minder) thumped him one – "Don't be stupid – of *course* he's not!" I said, "Don't thump him – he wants to know – questions should be answered." She was a hundred times more embarrassed than I was!'

In this mother's view, training for childminders was an important means for helping them to deal with situations such as this, concerning 'things you may not be able to answer out of your head – you might need some guidance'.

From what we have seen in our study, those responsible for the courses in Waltham Forest were making a committed, significant attempt to provide this. At the same time, it seemed that, with the resources available, they had merely stirred the surface of what are very deep waters.

The topic of racism was not addressed at all on the pre-registration course in Bracknell. When we raised it in our interviews with the sample childminders, all professed themselves to be non-racist in beliefs and practices. Disturbingly, however, their further comments indicated that their approach to dealing with different racial backgrounds among the children in their care would be to adopt a colour-blind perspective, which would 'show them that they are both the same really'. It was revealing to find that several Bracknell childminders also observed that the question of race was, as one put it:

'just not an issue here. It is in London because they're the vast majority in London... but not here.'

The implicit racist attitudes contained in such statements were reinforced by those with direct experience of what being part of a small minority ethnic group was like. One Bracknell mother, whose daughter was of mixed race described how:

'Bracknell is rife with (prejudice)... I've lost track of the hundreds of times that (child) has told me that somebody's called her names, pointed her out, hounded her, followed her... I always keep thinking I want to move back to London because I'm sick to death of it.'

The problem of racism in Britain makes the issue of immediate relevance for all who are responsible for the care and education of young children, irrespective of the racial composition of the community in which they happen to live. It is vital, therefore, that childminder training takes this on board in a way which will advance the development of childcare practice which recognises and values the differences among people from different backgrounds, and, at the same time, is founded upon the principle of equality.

Gender

Two of the mothers in the study stated explicitly that they wanted a childminder who was anti-sexist in her views on child-rearing. For example, one mother, who saw the caregiver as a significant role model, did not want a childminder who, in her words, adopted a 'little wifey' role.

'I don't want my daughters to feel that when they leave school all that is open to them is to have babies and keep house.'

The treatment of boys and girls was addressed during the sessions on children's play on the pre-registration courses in each area, although in a rather more forceful manner in the London borough, where reference was made to the authority's commitment to gender equality. A group exercise was carried out on the Waltham Forest course, to consider characteristics conventionally attributed to girls and boys. The ensuing discussion revealed clear indications of gender stereotyping amongst the participants and traditional sex roles in their own family lives, which were, however, not explored any further during the discussion. With regard to play provision, one course member described how her father-in-law had 'gone berserk' at the sight of her son playing with 'girls' toys. Another commented that she would be more likely to provide dolls if she was minding boys *and* girls rather than a boy on his own.

Similarly, in Bracknell, a discussion of the way in which boys and girls are brought up elicited comments from participants such as: 'You shouldn't stop boys playing with girls' toys – they'll grow out of it!' – which went unremarked upon by the tutors.

During our interviews with the childminders in the sample, the view was unanimously expressed that boys and girls should have equal access to all types of toys and play activities. Just one example from our observation data, however, shows how much more subtle and insidious is the issue of gender stereotyping in day care.

Case 9

Two minded children, Kate and Neil, are playing Mummy and Daddy. The minder has been helping them to set up their 'house'.

Minder: You'd better cook your dinner, Kate.
Kate: I cook your dinner.
Minder: Hadn't you? Cook your dad some dinner?
Neil: I'm, I'm, I'm, the dad so I have to cook, O.K.?
Minder: (Laughs) Since when did the dads have to cook? (Laughs again) I think you've got that the wrong way. The mums cook, don't they?
Neil: Yes.
Minder: Well, I do anyway!

Here, the minder has stated a convention on what behaviour is considered appropriate for men and women. Such talk on her part may not be thought of explicitly as teaching, but the objectives, nevertheless, are similar: to inform the child of 'the way things are', thus reinforcing, rather than challenging, gender stereotypes.

By including the topic of gender on their course curriculum, the trainers in both our study areas were tackling an important issue for childcare. As with race and other sensitive subjects, however, they appeared to be avoiding the difficult task of progressing from what *is* to what *should be*. To do this effectively in respect of attitudes and behaviour which have long-established, deep roots requires considerable time and skill – not only to address childminders' own beliefs and practices, but to enable them to deal with the equally complex matter of parental perspectives. When one Waltham Forest course member asked how she should respond to parents' whose expectations reinforced gender stereotypes, the only suggestion was that she should explain to them that she provided a wide range of toys. Such a strategy would be unlikely to resolve the dilemma of one of the minders in our sample, who described how a father objected when his small son kissed the other minded boys goodbye: ' "Oh no, no!" he said – "You're not supposed to kiss boys!" '

In none of our sample cases, including those in which strong views had been expressed on the subject, had any discussion taken place between childminder and parent regarding respective views and practices in the treatment of boys and girls. As we have noted in respect of so many other aspects of childminding, it is important that training not only raises minders' awareness of the issues involved, but also stresses the need for communication between the various parties to a day care arrangement. It is only if the beliefs and practices which are important to each are made known to the other, that mutually satisfactory day care provision can be agreed and implemented.

Discussion

Quality in the field of children's day care is a complex and elusive concept. In exploring the nature of the experiences offered by the childminders in our study, we have deliberately sought to integrate a number of perspectives of what constitutes satisfactory provision. One of these, inevitably, was the childcare curriculum of the training courses in our two study areas, since childminder training formed the focus of our investigation. In addition, however, it was considered particularly important to incorporate the views of the providers and users of a day care service which, by operating largely in the world of private negotiation, enjoys little public consensus regarding what it should actually offer.

In describing the provision for the minded children in the study, we have sought to convey the overall reality of the day care setting, rather than dissect it into discrete elements of behaviour and interaction. The themes that we have explored through interview and observation thus refer to broad areas of activity and experience, namely:

- extending children's horizons;
- fostering social relations among children;
- forming an affectionate relationship in a secure environment;
- promoting racial and gender equality.

It is also important to acknowledge that the picture we have presented is not, and could not be, a complete one. In some cases, what parents or childminders described as the most vital component of good quality care – for example, that it should be 'as much like home as possible' – was, by definition, not *observable*. This is not, however, to deny its validity as a criterion of quality provision – just because the goals of day care may be diffuse, intangible and not easily accessible to empirical research, they should not be disregarded or lost from view.

From the information available to us, it appeared that the majority of the arrangements in our study were working, or had worked, to the satisfaction of all concerned, in terms of the quality of childcare which had been provided. In those cases in which one or more aspects of provision appeared less positive, there were indications that the characteristics and circumstances of parents *and* childminders introduced elements of stress and tension into the day care situation. Thus, while our findings support those of other researchers (for example, Goelman and Pence, 1987) in suggesting that 'low resource' families are likely to experience poorer quality day care, they also suggest that, in such cases, providers may also be characterised by disadvantage.

On the basis of our evidence, we must conclude that training attempts to influence childcare practice in the minding situation appeared to have made relatively little impact on its recipients. Given that the courses which we studied represented just brief introductions to the multi-faceted activity of childminding, this is, perhaps, hardly surprising. It might be argued that more focused, in-depth training initiatives would be more likely to produce change. Yet there are also cogent reasons for scepticism, at least with regard to the subject of childcare. The tendency for childminders to equate their caring role with mothering meant that their own parenting practice became the dominant influence on their approach to minded children. Since their beliefs and behaviour are likely to be long-established and deeply-rooted, this situation presents a major problem for those who seek to change childcare practice through the medium of childminder training.

This concerns whether minders' own parental values and practices are to be challenged in seeking to promote good quality childcare in the childminding setting. From the training we have observed in operation, there is at present little attempt to confront attitudes and behaviour which seem in conflict with what trainers are advocating, especially with regard to sensitive topics such as discipline, race and gender. The nub of this problem would seem to lie in the fact that childminding is also equated with mothering in the eyes of policy makers and professionals. Until the contradictions inherent in this view are recognised, and the provision of day care dissociated from parenting, it is difficult to see how training can create the perspectives needed for a new approach to childcare.

9. Postscript: endings and futures

Before drawing this account to a conclusion, it is revealing to look at what had happened, or was expected to happen, to our 30 childminding arrangements at the end of the fieldwork period. This highlights as much as anything else in the study both the positive and the negative aspects of childminding as it currently operates in this country.

We have already reported that half (15) of the placements had ended before the follow-up, approximately 10 months after the first interview. Although we were dealing with a relatively small, non-representative sample, this in itself seems a significant indicator of the instability of such day care arrangements, especially since the cases were deliberately selected on the expressed expectation of both parties that they would continue for the foreseeable future. Table 9.1 summarises the reasons given by the various respondents as to why the arrangements had been terminated.

Table 9.1 Reasons for the termination of placements

Ended by parents	*No of cases*
family moved	3
dissatisfaction with minder	2
mother had another baby	1
parent lost job	1
Ended by minder	
minder gave up minding:	
• to enter employment	4
• to study/train	2
minder unable to cover parent's changed working hours	1
	Total 14

(In one case, different reasons for termination were given by the minder, who was reported that it was due to the mother's pregnancy, and by the mother, who said that the minder had decided to get a job outside the home.)

Half of the terminated placements had been ended by the parents, and half by the childminders. Although only two of the reasons stated indicate obvious discontent, it appeared that problems with the arrangement were contributory causes in another couple of cases, in which the childminder had decided to give up day care and enter the labour market. In the other four cases in which the provider had ceased minding, the parents expressed their regret that a successful arrangement had ended and that they were obliged to find alternative care.

Although no general conclusions can be drawn from so small a sample, it should not go unremarked that no fewer than six out of the 30 childminders who had only months previously entered into an anticipated long-term care arrangement, had given up childminding altogether by the time of the follow-up. From the point of view of the parents and children who were reliant upon their services, such moves represented a break in continuity of care, the effects of which ranged from inconvenient to seriously problematic. On the providers' side, a variety of reasons underlay the apparently unexpected decision to stop childminding. These included negative motivation linked to dissatisfaction with current arrangements, as well as positive moves into other childcare work or training, for which the experience of childminding had provided a springboard.

All but two of the 15 continuing arrangements were expected to carry on for the foreseeable future. One of these represented a clear example of poor communication between the adults concerned, since the childminder expected the child to leave within a few months when she started nursery school, while the mother was planning that the arrangement would continue with an adjustment to the hours! In the second case, in Waltham Forest, the childminder expressed her willingness to provide care for as long as it was required, but the single mother concerned, although highly satisfied with the placement, was apprehensive that she might no longer be able to afford the fees: 'I get a subsidy now, but may not next financial year'. This case illustrates how achieving satisfactory day care depends not only upon the circumstances and characteristics of individual providers and consumers, but also on factors in the wider social context. In this instance, access to, and continuity of, provision was clearly linked to public policy and practice in the day care arena, particularly in terms of economic support.

In five of the remaining cases, the expectation on both sides was that the childminder would continue to look after the child in question after he or she entered school. In two instances, the parents had deliberately enrolled their children in the school attended by the minders' own children, in order to facilitate this arrangement. One mother expressed her delight with the situation.

'To be able to have that kind of continuity is wonderful – and the fact that (minder) is willing to make that commitment.'

Another mother, who was expecting a second child by the time of the follow-up interview, had arranged for her childminder to look after both children after her period of maternity leave. This mother, too, emphasised the importance of continuity of care.

'If (minder) said she couldn't have the other baby then I would seriously think of giving up work, because (child's) been with her such a long time and is so close to her that I wouldn't consider sending her to someone else.'

The closeness of the relationships which had developed in such cases, not only between minder and child, but between all members of the families concerned, had led to expectations that contacts would continue even after the arrangement ended. A minder who had looked after two children from the same family explained, 'you can't just sort of end four years like that and never see each other again'. The mother in the case expressed a similar view.

'I couldn't imagine ever losing contact – it's like (minder's) children are sort of cousins really.'

There is little doubt from the evidence of cases such as these that childminding can be a highly rewarding experience for all concerned. But, at the end of the study, we need to return to our initial question and ask: what contribution had childminder training made to these successful outcomes? In the final chapter, we shall review the evidence our findings have produced, and the implications for the future of training.

10. Can training make childminding work?

'A country's practices in the provision of child day care, including family day care, are embedded in its political beliefs regarding the relationship between government and individual, its economic beliefs regarding financing of services and its social beliefs regarding individual, family and community values.' (Deller, 1988)

Does training hold the key to transforming childminding into a high quality day care service, and a recognised occupation attracting due reward and status? It must be clear from the foregoing pages that there is no simple answer to such a question. To understand and assess the impact of childminder training, we need to look beyond its curriculum and manifest objectives to the social context in which it is delivered and received. It is also important to identify the different levels of this context as represented in the ecological model adopted for this study (see Chapter 3). This requires us to consider not only the relevant circumstances of the providers and users of childminding, but also the overarching political and ideological framework containing the dominant perspectives which influence the organisation of women's lives and the provision of day care.

The most significant structural influence on the way in which childminding operates – and thereby on the role and influence of training – is its location in the private sector of provision. As a home-based form of day care, childminding is of course characterised by privacy, in so far as it takes place away from public view and supervision. But this endemic feature is powerfully reinforced by a longstanding policy approach which accepts a limited role for the public authorities in regulating the terms and conditions under which childminding is conducted, and the nature of the childcare which it provides.

Official involvement in childminding in Britain is at its most forceful at the point of provider registration. Legislation requires numerous checks on applicants and their homes, in the interest of child protection. Thereafter, however, public intervention in the form of supervision and support of childminding takes place within the considerably less forceful framework of guidelines to local authorities. Great variation exists between social services depart-ments in respect of such matters as home visits to childminders by advisory staff, and the provision of training and support facilities. This no doubt reflects the relative importance accorded to child-minding by an agency whose social work responsibilities make priority demands upon scarce resources. Even in areas of greatest development, however, there is little public involvement in the formation of childminding arrangements and in what takes place within them; aspects which, as far as providers and users are concerned, are what childminding is really all about.

A typical childminding placement thus brings together two families, in most cases strangers to each other, to negotiate between themselves both the form and content of an arrangement involving the intimate and emotive matter of the care of a young child. As our study has shown, this could be a discomforting, if not daunting, experience for both parties. Parents, often struggling with ambivalent feelings about using day care at all, sought to reassure themselves that their children would be happy and well cared for, while childminders were anxious to gauge whether the youngsters concerned would fit in to their family setting. At the same time, each party experienced some apprehension as to whether the other would adhere to the formal terms of the arrangement which was being agreed. Since none of these outcomes could be predicted with any certainty at the outset, embarking upon a childminding arrangement under these circumstances involved a strong element of risk, and a successful placement depended heavily upon mutual trust, confi-dence and personal rapport. This being so, it was hardly surprising that 'luck' was the term most frequently mentioned by both childminders and parents in the study when pronouncing a verdict on their day care experiences.

A further consequence of a social policy which sets the activity of childminding firmly in the private domain is that, in contrast to the institutional characteristics of nursery care, there is no structural framework determining the form and content of the provision. In investigating the operation of childminding arrangements, therefore, we were concerned to identify the locus of control over what actually took place. Our findings indicated that, in all the major aspects of the arrangement – practical terms, personal relations and the nature of the day care provision – the balance of power tended to lie with the childminder. The main legitimising source of this power was the generally perceived territorial right to determine what goes on in one's own domestic environment. In many cases, however, this was augmented by the personal characteristics of the caregiver, in particular the perception of both parents and childminders of the latter's greater knowledge and experience of bringing up children.

Childminding has long been advocated by central government, policy makers and many professionals as the form of day care which, by virtue of its domestic setting, is best placed to meet the needs of young children. Also, as we have seen, many parents prefer childminding to group care because of its family-based informality and close personalised relationships. What seems to be less widely understood or acknowledged, however, is that it is essentially the *childminder's* home regime to which the minded child is exposed. As Clarke Stewart (1987) has noted:

'A family day care home is a home, even when it is stretched to take in more children. It functions as a home for the family who live there, and most providers strive to incorporate their young charges into their own family's routines, rather than making their home an institution.'

The greatest influence over a childminder's approach to day care provision is thus the shape and substance of her own family life. The perceived importance of being at home to care for her own family is a major reason for undertaking the work in the first place. The ages and dispositions of her own children may affect the type of day care arrangement she will accept, and their daily routine of school, meals and other activities will determine the pattern of the minded child's day. Above all, perhaps, it is the childminder's own parenting practice which governs her approach to the care experiences she provides. The almost universal claim by childminders that they treat minded children as their own has less to do with the affective or emotional content of the minder-child relationship, strong as this may be, than with the fact that, as far as childcare is concerned,

CAN TRAINING MAKE CHILDMINDING WORK?   191

minded children are subjected to the parenting values and behaviour of their caregivers.

This tendency is strongly reinforced by the equation of the role of childminder with that of parent. Such a perception has been strongly criticised by a number of researchers, who argue that the minder-child relationship is intrinsically different from that between child and parent (for example Bryant and others, 1980; Mayall and Petrie, 1983). Yet while the two relationships are clearly not equivalent, it is important not to disregard the empirical evidence, supported by the findings of this study, that both providers and users *do* perceive childminding as containing elements similar to mothering, and that this perception has a powerful influence on how childminding arrangements operate. For the success, or otherwise, of childminding placements is largely dependent on the extent to which two family systems are similar, or at least compatible. Where differences emerge in child-rearing practices and values, these become potentially problematic, since acknowledgement implies criticism or rejection of the other's approach to parenting. Our study has vividly illustrated the tensions created in the minder-parent relationship by this obstacle to open communication.

On the user side, it is reinforced by the perceived territorial and other prerogatives attaching to the provider, whereby many parents find it difficult to express their wishes, and even more to voice any disapproval, concerning their child's day care experience. But power does not reside wholly with the childminder in this respect, for our findings showed that they, too, hesitated to draw attention to differences in childcare practice, in the light of the perceived right of parents to bring up their children as they see fit. The outcome of this mutual inhibition was that fundamental beliefs regarding childcare were often not expressed explicitly, and arrangements proceeded on the assumption of shared values. When areas of disagreement became apparent, each side felt pressure to keep them covert, in order to avoid open conflict and its consequent threat to the continuation of the arrangement.

It is the inherent complexity and sensitivity of the adult relationships involved in childminding which, perhaps more than anything else, highlight the structural isolation in which this type of day care takes place, and the lack of external support in conducting their interaction in a manner conducive to satisfactory outcomes. As it stands, it is easy to see why so many participants in this study attributed the success of their arrangements to the fortuitous combination of like minds.

The contribution of training to successful arrangements

In the light of the above considerations, it was equally unsurprising to find that, as far as the key aspects of the arrangements were concerned – the personal relationships involved and the nature of the child care provision offered – the impact of childminder training had been quite negligible. This was in no way attributable to those directly responsible for its design and delivery; indeed, in both of the study areas, the childminding workers concerned showed great energy, skill and commitment in producing the modest courses which were possible given the limited resources available.

However, a major reason for the ineffectiveness of training initiatives lies in the structural and ideological framework surrounding childminding and the way in which the activity is perceived. A social policy which recognises little public responsibility for how childminding arrangements are actually conducted, and advocates childminding for its homelike qualities, allows for – and even encourages – the retention of the notion of childminding as substitute parenting. Given the sacrosanct privacy accorded to individual parenting practices in our society, trainers thus have no public value base regarding standards of childcare to support their efforts to address this topic and encourage change.

The result, as our study has shown, is that childminders are strongly resistant to the notion that, as mothers, they have anything to learn about how to provide for children. Trainers, themselves constrained by this dominant perception of the childminder's role, appear hesitant to venture too far into the minefield of diverse values and behaviour representing the parenting practice of course participants. Even where a local authority has a strong policy stance, as in Waltham Forest's laudable commitment to anti-racist and anti-sexist childcare, we have seen how difficult it was for trainers to confront clear indicators from course attenders that such approaches did not characterise their own home environment.

It is essential in our view that those responsible for childminding and childminder training grasp the nettle of clarifying the boundaries between what providers do as *parents* and what they should do as *caregivers*. Only then can the fundamental issue be addressed of what specific knowledge and skills childminders should possess in order to provide good quality care. It is also important to consider in this context how the role of childminder compares with that of others working with young children, and what implications this has for training. It is surely anomalous that while full-time training lasting two or four years is seen as necessary or desirable for employment in group settings, childminders, working in isolation and often with sizeable numbers of children (either together or consecutively) are deemed to require no more than a few hours' group discussion to prepare them for their task. It is worth noting the contrast with Sweden, where many municipalities require 50-100 hours introductory training for childminding, and the ultimate goal is for providers to receive training equivalent to that of a child nurse (Broberg and Hwang, 1991).

For such a change to occur, however, there needs to be a corresponding alteration in the way in which childminding is organised. We would argue that it needs to become more 'public' and lose its image of exclusively home-based care, in which the minded child's experience is indivisible from the family regime of the provider. One radical move which could draw childminding out of its private world and into public view would be the establishment of stronger links between childminders and institutional services for under-fives. Such measures have been proposed in very general terms in official documents (for example DHSS, 1978), but with little indication of their precise objectives or means of operation. We would envisage such a step as fulfilling a *training* function, and addressing the issue of the role of the childminder by focusing on the knowledge and skills required for work with young children, and on the overlap between the tasks of childminders and nursery workers.

In several areas, tentative steps in this direction have already been taken. In one of our study areas, Waltham Forest, pre-registration courses were held in day nurseries, and trainers sought to maintain the participants' links with the nursery through the provision of coffee mornings for childminders, during which minded children could take part in nursery activities. Other local authorities have experimented with various ways of attaching childminders to day nurseries in order to draw them into a network of pre-school services (Ferri and Birchall, 1987). For a number of reasons, however, we would not see day nurseries, or family centres as many have now become, as offering the optimal institutional link for childminders.

First, local authority provision is so limited that, in many areas, such opportunities would simply be unavailable. Secondly, its increasingly selective intake, and emphasis on therapeutic work with families perceived as problematic, makes it a less appropriate in-service training setting for the providers of mainstream day care. Having said that, such links could in fact prove beneficial to the increasing numbers of childminders caring for children placed with them by social services departments, children seen as having some priority need (Ferri and Birchall, 1987).

Given the desire of many parents for their children to experience pre-school education (for example, Hughes and others, 1980), there would seem to be a strong case for attaching childminders, wherever possible, to a local nursery school or class. Depending on the numbers involved, childminders could be expected to spend one or more sessions a week as co-workers in the nursery setting, which would function as a learning environment, affording the opportunity to acquire knowledge and skills relevant to the promotion of children's development. Such an arrangement would be particularly advantageous in the light of the impending introduction of National Vocational Qualifications, in which childminding is to be included (Hevey, 1990). Under this system, qualifications are to be awarded largely on the basis of observed performance in the work role. As long as childminding is carried on solely in the privacy and isolation of the home setting, the problems of effective assessment of their work are clearly considerable.

Linking childminders to nursery education establishments would obviously require careful thought, planning and negotiation. Nursery places would need to be available for any children in the minder's care; the skills required by nursery staff and the demands placed upon them as informal trainers would have to be properly recognised and resourced. Against this, however, there would be a corresponding benefit to the institution of additional adult help from skilled and, hopefully, motivated workers. Such an arrangement would not necessitate any abrogation of social services' current responsibility for childminding; advisory workers could themselves establish links with the schools concerned to monitor the progress of minded children in a way not feasible at present, and to offer continued supervision and support to the childminders.

Linking childminders to the educational system would not, however, meet all of the training needs attaching to their work. As far as childcare and development are concerned, nursery schools and classes have little or no remit in relation to the under-threes – arguably the age group for which training input is most needed. Also, even if such changes were to take place, the essence of childminding will continue to be home-based care in a family setting, and the personal relationships of those it brings together – both children and adults – will remain a major determinant of successful outcomes. Attaching childminders to nurseries would do little to address the sensitive issue of minder-parent interaction. Given this, perhaps the most important contribution which childminder train- ing, as currently organised, could make would be to equip providers to deal effectively with the difficult adult relationships which individual negotiation and interaction create. The combination of the formal and the personal in this relationship demands consider- able skill, self-awareness and sensitivity to the views and needs of others. Childminder training, in its present form, could concentrate more effectively in this area. At present, it hardly ventures beyond exhorting its listeners to practise good communication. Actually achieving this is no easy task, however, and childminders and parents alike would, as we have seen, benefit from help and support in dealing with this key aspect of their day care arrangements.

Can training make childminding a job?

Let us now consider the other sense in which we have used the term 'work' in this study, and look at the contribution of training towards endowing childminding with the occupational status to which its adherents aspire. The main thrust of training strategy in this area has been to encourage and equip childminders to conduct their activities more effectively as a self-employed business. Emphasis is laid on the need for explicit discussion and agreement with parents regarding the detailed terms of each arrangement, including its financial aspects, and the importance of recording everything in a formal contract. The areas of negotiation which childminders are urged to conduct on their own highlight not only the lack of structural support for their work, but also the ambiguous position in which training places the social services workers who deliver it. For such responsibility as they have for childminding extends to its users as well as its providers. Thus, while encouraging childminders to act in a way which will advance their own occupational interests, they also urge them to have regard for the needs and circumstances of parents in setting their terms for childcare. The dilemma this poses in terms of conflict of interest is, however, left to the childminder to resolve.

Our study provided some evidence that the above training messages were absorbed by recipients, at least to the extent of formalising the various terms and conditions of their arrangements. Here too, however, powerful structural and ideological forces acted to hinder any substantial moves towards elevating childminding to the rank of recognised occupation. Perhaps the most significant factor in this was economic. On the basis of our evidence, it is simply not possible for childminding to provide a viable income as long as the costs of day care are borne exclusively by parents. The private market context in which childminding operates is economically exploitative of both providers and users – while the rates of pay received by minders were, as we have seen, low by almost any standards, they nonetheless represented a costly outlay for many parents. Childminding, as it is currently organised, cannot guarantee an affordable service to its users, nor an adequate income to its providers.

The economic barrier to occupational status for childminding is reinforced by the pervasive ideology which associates home-based day care with the traditional domestic role of women, especially mothers. For both providers and users, the essence of childminding lies in the affective personal relationship between caregiver and child. This perception fits uneasily with the view of childminding as a formal business arrangement and the childminder's work as meriting calculated financial reward. To both parties, the notion that childminders should undertake their activities out of economic self-interest is anathema, and, as a result, the financial aspect of their arrangement becomes a source of tension and embarrassment. This is illustrated on the childminder's side by a tendency to disregard their financial rights to overtime or other additional payments. Such self-denial in practice contributes significantly to the smooth progress of the day care arrangement since our findings showed that, while parents expressed little criticism of basic charges, many resented the contractual provision for holiday pay, retainer fees and so on. Under such circumstances it is evident that when one or both parties to an arrangement are under financial pressure, the potential for stress and conflict is considerable.

Training which urges childminders to be more businesslike in their approach and, at the same time, emphasises the importance of the personal relationships involved, fails to acknowledge – and may actually even fuel – the contradictions inherent in the notion of childminding as an occupation. Yet it is clear that training cannot by itself resolve this contradiction, which has its roots in the broader social context in which childminding takes place. We would argue that the formal aspects of childminding arrangements need to be removed from the sphere of private negotiation between caregiver and parent, and established as part of a publicly regulated day care service. The controlling agency, most realistically social services departments, would be responsible for recruiting and employing providers on terms and conditions which give due recognition to the skills and responsibilities involved in providing home-based day care. Parental contribution to the costs of the service could be paid directly to the agency concerned, although other sources of funding would be required to ensure an adequate supply of high quality, affordable provision. In addition to an element of public funding, this could include an employers' contribution, possibly in the form of a pay roll tax as operated in Sweden (Broberg and Hwang, op. cit.). This would establish a principle of employer support for the family responsibilities of workers, and represent a more equitable distribution of such funding than the inevitably selective provision of workplace nurseries.

Perhaps more than any other single measure, such a move would elevate childminding to the status of a recognised occupation and, at the same time, contribute to solving what Moss (1990) has described as the day care 'trilemma', namely that of ensuring an adequate supply of good quality day care at costs that parents can afford and which offers satisfactory renumeration to providers. Furthermore, by removing private negotiation, it would create a climate more favourable to the development of positive minder-parent relationships, which would continue to be an essential ingredient of successful day care arrangements. It might also be argued that, since the costs to users would be reduced under such a system, parents would have considerable incentive to seek day care via official channels, and that the incidence of illegal, unregistered childminding would thus be markedly reduced.

If the foregoing arguments are insufficient to convince policy makers of the desirability of publicly regulated childminding, the implications of the demographic and labour market changes referred to at the beginning of this book may be more persuasive. Some years ago, Mayall and Petrie (1979) pointed out that:

'the promotion of childminding as a major form of day care rests on the assumption that... there remains a pool of women who are available to offer childcare and who do not seek or need proper recompense.'

The recent moves to encourage mothers of young children – the main suppliers of childminding – into employment may well alter the picture dramatically. Our own study has shown that a fifth of the providers involved had moved into employment or training within the space of a year. Similar trends elsewhere, especially in the United States, have led researchers to question whether the supply side of family-based day care may be in the process of dwindling away (for example Kamerman and Kahn, 1981).

It may be hypothesised that not only will childminders be in shrinking supply, but that the typical profile of such providers may also alter. An earlier return to the labour market may mean that childminding, if undertaken at all, is pursued for shorter periods, and more predominantly by women whose own children are very young. Such a trend would clearly have important implications for the future of childminding as the major source of day care for working parents. It would also raise a number of questions regarding the development of childminder training; including its purpose and effectiveness, and the resources needed to provide training for a group of practitioners characterised by increasingly high turnover.

Conclusion

Finally, to return to the *current* role of childminder training with which this study has been concerned, our findings have underlined the need to appraise its aims, methods and impact in the light of the broad social context in which it is being delivered. Contrary to what it would seem to suggest, the introduction of training by social services departments does not represent a major shift in the direction of public authorities taking responsibility for childminding and defining what it should provide.

This is largely because childminding takes place in a policy context which emphasises parental responsibility for child-rearing, and private arrangements as the solution to day care needs. Such a context offers no clear public value base from which standards of childcare can be derived, and no structure for promoting or protecting the status of childminders as workers. Under such circumstances, it is hardly surprising that the impact of the training initiatives which we have studied appeared to have been minimal; indeed our research has highlighted some of the fundamental contradictions which emerge when a public agency seeks to train for an activity for which it accepts little other responsibility. For childminding to be amenable to change through training, there must first of all be a change in the way childminding is organised. The problems and paradoxes identified within the training programmes which have been studied here symbolise the shortcomings of a day care service which operates to such a large extent within the domain of privacy.

A more fundamental issue is at stake here, however, concerning the boundaries of societal and parental responsibility for children. The prevailing system rests upon a dominant ideology which defines children as belonging to their parents rather than to society as a whole. As a result, a great deal of what happens to children is left to the vagaries of private responses to meeting their needs.

Having undertaken this detailed study of how childminding operates, we would conclude that what is required is a reappraisal at the highest level of social policy concerning the nature of public responsibility for young children and their development, and within this, how childminding and other forms of day care are provided. For childminding in particular, only a move in the direction of greater social responsibility for the provision of a high quality service can help ensure that it makes a positive contribution to the well-being and development of all children who experience it, and that those who undertake the skilled and demanding task of providing such care will receive due recognition and reward.

References

Association of Advisers for the Under Fives for England and Wales. *Research Report of the Nurseries and Childminders Regulation Act 1948.* 1980.

Association of County Councils and Association of Metropolitan Authorities. Inter-association Working Party: Provision for Under Fives. *Under Fives: A Local Authority Associations' Study.* 1977.

Beckwith, J., *Training and Support in Childminding – a national response*: 1982.

Belsky, J., 'Future directions for day care research: an ecological analysis.' in *Child Care Quarterly*, vol. 9, Part 2, 82–89: 1980.

Belsky, J. and Steinberg, L., 'The effects of day care: a critical review' in *Child Development*, vol. 49, 929–949: 1978.

Belsky, J., Steinberg, L. and Walker, A., 'The ecology of day care' in Lamb, M. (Ed.), *Childminding in Non-traditional Families, Hillsdale, NJ*, Erlbaum: 1982.

Berridge, D. and others, Report for the Open University on the evaluation of the pilot phase of P653 'Caring for children and young people', University of Bristol, Dartington Social Research Unit: 1985.

Bone, M., *Preschool Children and the Need for Day Care*, London, HMSO: 1977.

Bowlby, J., *Maternal Care and Mental Health*, Geneva, WHO: 1952.

Brannen, J. and Moss P., *New Mothers at Work*, London, Unwin Hyman: 1988.

Broberg, A. and Hwang, C. Philip, 'Day care for young children in Sweden' in Melhuish E.C. and Moss P., *Day Care For Young Children: International Perspectives*, Tavistock/Routledge, London and New York: 1991.

Bronfenbrenner, U., 'Towards an experimental ecology of human development' in *American Psychologist*, 32, 513-31: 1977.

Bryant, B., Harris, M. and Newton, D., *Children and Minders*, Grant McIntyre: 1980.

Challis, L., *The Great Under Fives Muddle: Options for Day Care Policy*, University of Bath, School of Humanities and Social Services: 1980.

Clarke Stewart, A., 'Predicting Child Development from Child Care Forms and Features, – the Chicago Study', and 'In Search of Consistencies in Child Care Research, in Philips, D.A. *Quality in Child Care: What Does Research Tell Us?* Research Monographs of the National Association for the Education of Young Children Vol. 1: 1987

Clarke Stewart, K.A. and Fein, G., *Early Childhood Programs*: 1983.

Cohen, B., *Caring for children: Report for the European Commission's Childcare Network*, Commission of the European Communities, London: 1988.

Community Relations Commission, *Who Minds? A Study of Working Mothers and Childminding in Ethnic Minority Communities*: 1975.

Davie, C., *An Investigation of Childminding in North Staffordshire*, Report to DHSS: 1986.

Deller, J., *Family Day Care Internationally: A Literature Review*, Toronto, Ontario Ministry of Community and Social Services: 1988.

Department of Health, 'The Care of Children Principles and Practice' in *Regulations and Guidance*, London, HMSO: 1991

Department of Health and Social Security, *Children's Day Care Facilities at 31 March 1986*: 1986.

Department of Health and Social Security, *Children's Day Care Facilities at 31 March 1976*: 1976.

Department of Health and Social Security, LASSL Circular 78 (1): 1978.

Department of Health and Social Security, Department of Education and Science, *Low Cost Day Provision for the Under Fives*, DHSS: 1976.

Ferri, E. and Birchall, D., *A Study of Support and Training Services for Childminders*, National Children's Bureau: 1984.

Ferri, E. and Birchall, D., *Changing Childminders*, National Children's Bureau: 1987.

Ferri, E and Birchall, D., *Follow up Study of Support and Training Services for childminders*, National Children's Bureau: 1987a.

Ferri, E. and Saunders, A., *Parents, Professionals and Pre-school Centres*, National Children's Bureau/Barnardo's: 1991.

Ferri, E. and Stern, L., *An Evaluation of an Innovative Childminding Support Scheme*. National Children's Bureau: 1987.

Georgiades, N.J. and Phillimore, L., 'The myth of the hero-innovator and alternative strategies for organisational change' in Kiernan C.C. and Woodford P.F. (Eds) *Behaviour Modification with the Severely Retarded*. Associated Scientific Publishers, Amsterdam, Oxford, New York: 1975.

Gittins, D., *The Family in Question*, Macmillan: 1985.

Goelman, H. and Pence, A.R., 'Effects of child care, family and individual characteristics on children's language development: the Victoria Day Care Research Project', in Philips, D.A.(Ed.) *Quality in Child Care: What Does Research Tell Us?* Research Monographs of the National Association for the Education of Young Children. Vol.1: 1987.

Henwood, M., Rimmer, L. and Wicks, M., *Inside the Family*, Family Policy Studies Centre: 1987.

Hevey, D., *Working with Under Sevens Project. Final Report*, Care Sector Consortium. 1990.

Honig, A., 'Research: A tool to promote optimal early child care and education' in *Early Child Development and Care*, vol. 33. 1988.

Howe, D., 'A Framework for understanding evaluation research in social work' in *Research, Privacy and Planning*, Vol. 5, No. 2: 1988.

Hoy, J. and Kennedy, M., 'Women's paid labour in the home,' in Simpson and Simpson *Research in the Sociology of Work*: 1983.

Hughes, M., Moss, P., Perry, J., Petrie, P. and Pinkerton, G., *Nurseries Now: A Fair Deal For Parents and Children*, Penguin: 1980.

Jackson, B., *Changing Childminders*, National Elfrida Rathbone Society: 1979.

Jackson, B and Jackson, S., *Childminder: a study in Action Research*, Routledge and Kegan Paul. 1979.

Kamerman, S., and Kahn, A., *Childcare, family benefits and working parents. A study in comparative policy*, USA, Columbia University Press: 1981. (Comparative study of policies in France, Hungary, German Democratic Republic and Sweden.)

Katz, D. and Kahn, R.L., *The Social Psychology of Organisations*, New York, Wiley: 1966.

Land, H. and Parker, R., 'United Kingdom' in Kamerman, S.B. and Kahn, A.J., *Family Policy: Government and Family in 14 Countries*, New York, Columbia University Press: 1978.

Lane, S., 'Women and childcare: factors influencing social work dealings in Women's lives' in *British Journal of Social Work*, vol. 16, Supplement: 1986.

Martin, J. and Roberts, C., *Women and Employment: a Lifetime Perspective*, London, HMSO: 1984.

Mayall, B. and Petrie, P., *Minder, Mother and Child*, University of London Institute of Education: 1977.

Mayall, B. and Petrie, P., *Childminding and Day Nurseries: What kind of Care?* Heineman Educational Books: 1983.

Melhuish E.C. and Moss, P., *Day Care for Young Children: International Perspectives*, Tavistock/Routledge, London and New York. 1991.

Ministry of Health Circular 5/65

Ministry of Health Circular 37/68

Morrison, A. and McIntyre, D., 'Changes in opinion about education in the first year of teaching in *British Journal of Clinical Psychology* 6, 161–163: 1967.

Moss, P., *A Review of Childminding Research*, Thomas Coram Research Unit. Working and Occasional Paper No. 6: 1990.

Moss, P., 'Work, family and the care of children: issues of equality and responsibility', in *Children and Society*, vol. 4, No. 2. 1990.

Musgrave, P.W., *The Sociology of Education*, Methuen: 1972.

National Childminding Association, *Working Party Report on the Law*: 1979.

National Childminding Association, *The Law on Childminding; Discussion Paper on Good Practice*: 1984.

Open University/National Childminding Association, *Childminding: Materials for Learning and Discussion*: 1986.

Owen, S., 'The 'unobjectionable' service: a legislative history of childminding, in *Children and Society (1988–9)*, 4, 367–382: 1989.

Philips, D.A., *Quality in Child Care: What Does Research Tell Us?* Research Monographs of the National Association for the Education of Young Children Vol. 1: 1987.

Philips, D.A. and Howes, C., 'Indicators of quality child care: review of research in Philips, D.A. (above): 1987.

Piaget, J., *Origin of Intelligence in the Child*, Penguin: 1977.

Powell, D.R., The role of research in the development of the child care profession in *Child Care Quarterly* 11(1): 1982.

Pugh, G., Aplin, G., De'Ath, E. and Moxon, M., *Partnership in Action: Working with Parents in Pre-school centres*, National Children's Bureau: 1987.

Pugh, G. and De'Ath, E., *Working Towards Partnership in the Early Years*, National Children's Bureau. 1989.

Patton, M.Q., *Qualitative Evaluation Methods*, Sage Publications Inc.: 1980.

Ruopp, R., Travers, J., Glantz, F. and Coelen, C., *Children at the Centre: Final Results of the National Day Care Study*, Cambridge MA. Abt. Associates: 1979.

Sylva, K., Smith, T. and Moore, E., *Monitoring the High/Scope Training Programme 1984–1985. Final Report*: 1986.

Taylor, S.J. and Bogdan, R., *Introduction to Qualitative Research Methods*, John Wiley and Sons: 1984.

Tizard, J., Moss, P. and Perry, S., *All Our Children*, London, Temple Smith/New Society: 1976.

Trades Union Congress Report, *Charter On Facilities For the Under Fives*: 1979.

Van der Eyken, W., *Day Nurseries in Action*, University of Bristol, Child Health Research Unit: 1984.

Van der Eyken, W., *The DHSS Under-fives Initiative 1983–1987. Final report*, Department of Health and Social Security: 1987.

Wagner Report, *Report of the Independent Review of Residential Care*, National Institute for Social Work, London, HMSO: 1988.

Working for Childcare, *Meeting the Childcare Challenge: Can the Market Provide?*: 1990.

Index

children, minded *cont*

social development 162-174
in this study, profiled 59-67
needs 12-13
numbers 1
relationships
with adults 135-40,187
with minders' children
87,120-21,141-2,158,168
Children Act, 1989: 3,4,5,29-30,56
class, social 32,64,146-7
see also costs
communication 123-30
see also relationships
conflict between minders and parents
127-31,135-9,174,191
see also relationships
contracts
advice to parents 53
generally 93-8
in training programmes 46,84-5,195
safeguard minders' interests 109,110
corporal punishment 55,121,128
costs of childminding 99-109,186-7,196-7
subsidised 45,186-7
see also business aspects; class
criticism
of minders by parents, suppressed
128-31,174,191
of parents by minders, implied 68-9,131-5
see also relationships
cultural issues 4,22,52-3,178
see also minority ethnic groups; race
day care, status of 24,37-8,41,197
demographic change 8-9,197-8
dissatisfaction of parents
termination of arrangements 140-41,185-6
with care offered 156-8,167-9,172-3,174-5
with relationship with minder
127-31,135-9,174,191
see also relationships
drop-in centres 157,160-62,165,167

E,F
economic
aspects of minding *see* costs
pressure on demand for minders 8-9,15
education *see* nursery education
emotional aspects of relationships
conflict with business aspects
102-9,112-3,117-8,196
in initial contacts 78-91
in ongoing arrangements

emotional aspects of relationships *cont*

minder/child 136-8,170-74
minder/parent 116-35
training on 42
valued 187
employers
demand for minding 8
financial contribution to future provision
197
responsibility to facilitate minding 9,13-14
employment
minding as 109-14,195-8; *see also* business
aspects
of minders by local authorities
5-6,38,113-14,197
of mothers in this study 64-9
of women 7-9,10-11,16,198
ethnic groups, minority *see* minority ethnic
groups
Europe 7,9
Sweden 193,197
experience of minders, parents' deference to
131-4
families
differences in minders' and parents'
assumptions 127-30
in this study, profiled 59-73
minders' 190-91
see also parents
family
context of childcare 10-11
context of minding, valued 70-71,183; *see
also* privacy
freedom from government control 11-13
opportunities for social interaction in
163-70
see also parents
fathers
domestic responsibilities 11-12,66-7
in this study 61,64
interviews 33
involvement with minders 123
see also gender issues; parents
feminism 9
see also gender issues
finance *see* business aspects; costs; economic
pressure
First Aid 42,51,175-6

G,H,I
gender issues 46,49,180-82
see also fathers
government *see* central government; local
authorities